Scarecrow Studies in Young Adult Literature
Series Editor: Patty Campbell

Scarecrow studies in Young Adult Literature is intended to continue the body of critical writing established in Twayne's Young Adult Authors Series and to expand it beyond single-author studies to explorations of genres, multicultural writing, and controversial issues in YA reading. Many of the contributing authors of the series are among the leading scholars and critics of adolescent literature, and some are YA novelists themselves.

The series is shaped by its editor, Patty Campbell, who is a renowned authority in the field, with a thirty-year background as critic, lecturer, librarian, and teacher of young adult literature. Patty Campbell was the 2001 winner of the ALAN Award, given by the Assembly on Adolescent Literature of the National Council of Teachers of English for distinguished contribution to young adult literature. In 1989 she was the winner of the American Library Association's Grolier Award for distinguished service to young adults and reading.

Beyond the Pale

New Essays for a New Era

Marc Aronson

*Scarecrow Studies in Young Adult
Literature, No. 9*

The Scarecrow Press, Inc.
Lanham, Maryland, & Oxford
2003

SCARECROW PRESS, INC.

Published in the United States of America
by Scarecrow Press, Inc.
A Member of the Rowman & Littlefield Publishing Group
4720 Boston Way, Lanham, Maryland 20706
www.scarecrowpress.com

PO Box 317
Oxford
OX2 9RU, UK

Library of Congress Cataloging-in-Publication Data

Aronson, Marc.
  Beyond the pale : new essays for a new era / Marc Aronson.
    p. cm.— (Scarecrow studies in young adult literature ; 9)
  Includes bibliographical references and index.
  ISBN 0-8108-4638-1 (hardcover : alk. paper)
  1. Young adult literature, American—History and criticism. 2. September 11
Terrorist Attacks, 2001—Literature and the terrorist attacks. 3. Teenagers—
Books and reading—United States. 4. Pluralism (Social sciences)—United
States. I. Title. II. Series.
  PS490 .A76 2003
  810.9'9283—dc21

                                                        2002151299

To teenagers, in the hope that adults talking and writing about you may enable us to do a better job of providing you with great books, and great ideas.

Contents

Acknowledgments

This book of essays was created during a twelve-month period beginning just before September, 2001, a particularly difficult year for all Americans. When I wrote the essay that begins the book and published it in *Horn Book*, I knew it would inspire controversy. But, despite what many have thought, my aim was not to be the bad boy creating havoc in class, but to enter into an important conversation with my peers, people I respect. Many of those reviewers, librarians, authors, editors, and teachers did respond to that essay, both in print and in person. Most disagreed with me, disagreements that took on particular resonance in a year when all of us had to reconcile our bonds and our differences.

I would like to thank those interrogators whose questions and challenges were particularly helpful to me in defining my own beliefs: Rita Auerbach, Eliza Dresang, Nikki Giovanni, Joanna Rudge Long, Walter Dean Myers, Roger Sutton, Henrietta Smith, Deborah Taylor, and my wife, Marina Budhos. I am grateful that they, and many others, took my ideas seriously enough to disagree fervently in some cases, question deeply in others, and always to force me to examine my own beliefs and sharpen my conclusions. I am particularly pleased that Andrea Davis Pinkney allowed me to include her essay, written in response to mine, in this collection. While we have disagreed in person and in print, this exchange has only given us a better chance to get to know each other.

I am also grateful to Patty Campbell for being an enthusiastic and yet probing editor and giving me this extended forum for my ideas. Her detailed knowledge of the history of YA books and their readers is always a salutary check to my tendency to make historical generalizations.

Earlier versions of some of the chapters in this book appeared in the following places. The author thanks the original publishers for their cooperation and, where relevant, permission to use the previously published essays in this volume.

Chapter 1: *Horn Book,* May/June 2001.
Chapter 2: *Horn Book,* Sept./Oct. 2001, copyright Andrea Davis Pinkney
Chapter 4: Speech to the Alliance for Arts Education, New Jersey Lawrenceville Arts Center, October 16, 2001.
Chapter 5: Speech to the Reading Excellence Through the Arts Program at the International Reading Association Convention, San Francisco, April 29, 2002.
Chapter 6: *School Library Journal,* November 2001.
Chapter 7: Speech to the Middle East Institute, Columbia University, April 4, 2002.
Chapter 9: *Features,* Children's Book Council, Vol. 54, No. 1, Spring 2001.
Chapter 10: Speech to the Children's Book Guild, Washington, D.C. May 23, 2002.
Chapter 12 *Youth Services Manual,* Illinois Young Adult Library Association, 2002.
Chapter 14: Speech to a conference on nonfiction, Children's Literature Network, Minnesota.
Chapter 15: Speech to Childrens Literature New England, Massachusetts, August 8, 2002.

Introduction

The One and the Many:
Of Hedgehogs and Foxes

The British philosopher Isaiah Berlin wrote one of the most famous essays of the twentieth century, "The Hedgehog and the Fox." Berlin had been born in Russia before the revolution. He was not sympathetic to the claims of groups, such as the Communists and the Fascists, who seemed to have one single great truth they insisted on inflicting on the world. But in London and Paris he found many intellectuals who did find those grand ideas, those ideologies, congenial. In fact most of his peers were contemptuous of him for refusing to see the big truths. They thought that lurking behind every human opinion, idea, insight, yearning were larger forces such as class, race, or gender that simple folk refused to acknowledge. These determining conditions and how people reacted to them informed and deformed all of their thought. Unless you addressed the big underlying issues you were no intellectual.

Berlin had a different view. He divided the world into two types of people, hedgehogs and foxes. As the Greek poet Archilochus had put it, "the fox knows many things, but the hedgehog knows one big thing." Hedgehogs, like his opponents, had one single idea, one channel, in which they kept burrowing. Foxes, like Berlin, scampered here and there collecting many interesting bits, never needing to turn them into a single grand idea. Berlin, like the French philosopher Raymond Aron, was condemned for being soft, too accepting of simplistic middle-class ideas that did not challenge the true structures of power. But after the fall of the Soviet Union in 1989, many thinkers looked back at Berlin and Aron and realized that they had been right. Truth may not rest in some grand theory but rather may glint and sparkle in the many small insights and ideas that come to us daily.

The obvious touchstone for this collection of essays is chapter one, "Of Slippery Slopes and Proliferating Prizes," an essay which first appeared in the May/June 2001 issue of the *Horn Book* and drew more mail than any article in the history of the magazine. In one sense I was inspired by Berlin in resisting the grand architecture of much of the discussion in children's books—the focus on the race, gender, or ethnicity of its creators and readers. But in another I was being precisely a hedgehog. I was claiming that there is a grand and transcendent thing called art, or literary distinction, which does not come down to the many separate truths of hyphenated distinction. This was a point a number of my critics raised when they responded to the *Horn Book* with letters to the editor. They stressed the standards of quality that, for example, the Coretta Scott King Awards observe.

I was well into writing a response to those critics when the attacks of September 11, 2001, took place. I decided that in view of the tragedy, hashing over the issues was petty. But now, more than a year later, I will take the opportunity to revisit those issues and to recast the question in terms that hearken back to Berlin's essay, and also define the themes of this book.

THE PALE

My father, Boris Aronson, was born in Kiev just before the start of the twentieth century, when it was part of the empire of the Romanovs. As a Jew, he could only live and work in certain specified parts of the country, called the Pale of Settlement. He experienced pogroms, and his father played an important role in one particularly telling expression of anti-Semitism. My grandfather was a rabbi, as had sixteen generations of my forbears been before him.

But he knew Russian and was in touch with the surrounding world. When a man named Mendel Beilis was arrested in Kiev, the rabbi helped organized the committee for his defense.

As readers of Bernard Malamud's novel *The Fixer* know, Beilis had been accused of ritual murder, of killing a young Christian boy to use his blood in monstrous Jewish rites. This so-called "blood libel" was an accusation against Jews that had first been made in Norwich, England, in 1144, and had moved slowly eastward across Europe. It is still muttered today on the Internet and in anti-Semitic literature. But the Beilis case was the last official stand of this particular strand of institutionalized anti-Semitism, for with the support of able lawyers and an aroused community a Russian jury handpicked to condemn Beilis instead found him innocent. He then followed my grandfather's suggestion to leave for Palestine.

My father's childhood legacy was the clash between the world of deadly superstition and the modern world. Modernity entered his life in another way, too. Religious Jews were forbidden to draw anything figurative, since they might be capturing the aspect of God. But when my father was a little boy in religious school, he drew a fly on the side of the page, and the teacher swatted and swatted away at it, until he realized what the mischievous boy had done. That was only the start of his transgression. When he got older and began to learn about the experiments in art that were taking place in Paris, he became obsessed.

My father did not support the political revolution of the Bolsheviks. He had his fill of politics one terrifying night when some self-proclaimed revolutionary commissars appointed him to guard a jail filled with large, frightening prisoners. And watching surly, coarse Bolsheviks arrest a captured aristocrat he had the sense that the grace and bearing of the gentlemen made him the leader, not the prisoner, of the mob. Utopian phrases in mouths of drunken ruffians were no path to freedom.

But my father enthusiastically supported the artistic revolutions taking place all around him. Even before the revolution he went to study with a leading constructivist, Alexandra Exter, and penniless, he left the Pale to take the dangerous journey to Moscow to see the amazing artwork owned by Sergai Shchukin. This famous collector was a patron of Matisse and the postimpressionists, and visiting his home was the only way an aspiring Russian artist could see the most advanced art in the world. The collection was only open to the public on Sundays. By the laws of the Tsar it was illegal for my father, a Jew, to be in Moscow at all. By the laws of his faith, he could not travel on Saturday, the Sabbath.

My father could not resist the promise of seeing the new art. He arrived during the week when the Shchukin home was closed to the public. The doorman told him to go away and return on Sunday. My father was sleeping in a stable, and could certainly not risk hiding out in Moscow for days waiting for his chance. He pleaded that he was a student of Exter's, and of his passion for the art. Shchukin himself overheard his fervent words, and showed him around the collection.

Modern art, art that broke boundaries and pushed for new truth, was so important to my father that he left everything he knew, risked everything, just to see it. He went on to follow the lead of other Jewish artists such as Marc Chagall in inventing a new Jewish art, built on its folk traditions but fully modern in its abstract style. Then he immigrated to America, leaving behind the Pale, the pogroms, and the grand idea of Communism that would sweep both away.

This story, sort of the founding legend of my family, links Berlin's essay and my controversy with the world of children's literature. Jewish art that is true to its roots would be a nonfigurative art, a folk art of decorative borders and illustrated manuscripts. Jewish art as it exploded into the world at the turn of the last century joined the grand big idea of modern art, abstract art. It left behind its roots to become part of the language of the world—as my father did by working on Broadway, and as so many of his peers did in Hollywood.

In its focus on authenticity, I believe the children's world wants to keep its works as a kind of folk art—true to its traditions, recognizable to its readers, confirming of the values of the community that creates it. That is the art of the Pale of Settlement. The blood libel, for that matter, was a folk belief, deeply held by many peasants. Challenging it was a rejection of oral traditions and shared beliefs. It was a triumph of modernity.

Those who favor authenticity of the folk art variety are, you might say, foxes. Each group has its own art, and readers hop, skip, and jump among them. The idea of the modern was that artists could dip into these folk styles, but transform them with the eyes of the new world of machines, films, airplanes. If we want to claim that books for younger readers are truly an art form, not a craft, not a folk art, we need a similar commitment to a big idea. We have to accept that it is standards that rule, not communities.

That is the big idea behind this collection: I ask in many different ways, "What is the truth of the universal, the general, the claim of art and ideas to cut through difference and apply to all?" And, in reverse, "What is the claim of the particular, the small, the individual resisting a grand truth imposed—perhaps with the best of intentions—by rabbis, priests, mullahs, critics, or governing boards?"

While the terrorist attacks dissuaded me from immediately publishing a lengthy defense of my essay on the prizes, I also think they make these big questions all the more important. The driving force behind fundamentalists throughout history—just like the Communists and Fascists Berlin opposed—is to create a utopia, a perfected society, by eliminating error. While part of the necessary response to that is military strength, another element must be a moral strength of our own, in which we define ever more clearly to ourselves where we see the roots of a better future. If it is not in perfection, the grand idea imposed by the devout, it must be in the particular, the uncertain, the oddball visions of individuals. So if on the one hand the art I take a stand for is the big universal of standards against the folk-art particularities of communities, it is also the strangeness of individual creations against rules for children and art, set outside of the artistic process.

In putting together this collection, I noticed something else about my writing and thinking this year: the importance of religion. This was a year of conflicts cloaked in religious terms, but also of renewed religious feeling. Though, like my father, I am not a devout Jew, it is clear to me that Judaism, and religion more generally, is present in much of my thinking. Maybe this is the essence of what modernism did for my family; it said that you need not lose your heritage by embracing ideas that come from others. There was nothing good about the Pale. It is not restriction that nurtures our heritages. Rather our traditions grow, change, and take on new life when we let in the fresh air of the surrounding world. Paris gave my father his artistic vocabulary, but his work was no less Jewish for that. My orientation is entirely secular, and relentlessly Talmudic.

Part of my contention with the children's community comes, I think, because of a difference in who we face every day. When they read a book, librarians see the faces of the kids, parents, and teachers they serve. A book, we often hear, is a tool. A librarian is eager to have something to give to a particular reader, who wants to see her own face, or her own story, or a book that will help him, or that he will love. I, on the other hand, see the author, the weirdness of the artist's invention. I am not focused on the utility of the book, but on opening up the process of creation so the author has the greatest freedom to find his true voice.

Or at least that is half true. The higher you rise in the publishing ladder, the more Janus-faced your vision becomes: I face both the author and the buying public and must please both. Part of the reason for writing essays such as those in this book is to build a bridge between those two groups, the creator and the buyer. This double vision becomes even more complex when the assumed readers are teenagers, with their own strong, but generally ignored, views on books. I discuss the special YA publishing challenges in section four, and especially in chapter eleven, "Teenagers Don't Want to Read about Teen Angst, So Why Are So Many Angst-Filled Books Published?"

HISTORY

On September 11, 2001, history crashed into all of our lives. We joined people who were adults in 1963, and 1941, and 1929, and in all other such key moments in becoming the sort of person who, from now on, will be asked, "Where were you when you heard?" Part of the reason that this was such a powerful event for Americans is that we have felt immune to history. Historians often point out that only those who have experienced American history as a set of losses—Indians, African Americans, southern whites—have a real sense of the weight of the past. The rest of us have tended to look ahead, to the future. The terrorist attacks reminded us that there are those in the world with longer memories, while they also placed an indelible mark on our own historical imagination.

I mention this because throughout this year I found that history shaped my thinking. I turned to the past to understand the present, as in chapters six and seven on the Puritans and modern Islamic fundamentalists. But I also kept pondering how we should teach and write history for younger readers as in chapters eight, "*The Crucible*: Witch-Hunt and Religion, Crossing Point of Many Histories," nine, "Biography and Its Perils," ten, "The Pursuit of Happiness: Does American History Matter?" and fourteen, "Woke Up, Got Out of Bed, Dragged a Comb across My Head: Is the Past Knowable?" I came to recognize that throughout my disagreements with my colleagues in the world of children's literature I seek to challenge their sense of speaking for timeless categories such as "Children" and "Literature" and "Authenticity." I keep wanting to say, no, you are speaking about a particular moment for a discrete set of historical reasons. And if you are, then everything you say is subject to change. This is a main point of the longest essay in the book, "Am I My Brother's Keeper?" which also makes up its last chapter.

NONFICTION AND BOY READERS

The historical sensibility is also expressed in another theme in this book. If my essay on prizes and responses to the terrorist attacks gave rise to two sets of essays, a third follows on from the new interest in nonfiction that seems to be spreading in the world of books for younger readers. The Robert L. Sibert Prize not only gave a boost to nonfiction, it recognized the potential of the field. In the sixties and seventies—in the wake of Soviet space achievements that made Americans fear we were falling behind in science, as well as American successes that made science seem glamorous—there was a burst of interest in nonfiction for children. While the publishing of books on natural history

has puttered along well enough since then and had one spectac-
ular if unrepeatable triumph in the development of the Eyewit-
ness style of books, more recently nonfiction fell into a duller
pattern.

Here again events press in on us. The changed world we live
in demands that we, at all ages, know more about the world
around us, the peoples with whom we share the planet. Immigration is radically changing the face of America, which gives us
new reasons to reexamine our history and to see the links and
parallels we have had with others in the past. As we all function
in a digital world characterized by daily technological change,
science and math are just so interesting and relevant that our industry simply must find new ways to present them to young
people. It is our resistance that is out of step with their world.

This resistance has dire consequences. In my first collection of
essays, *Exploding the Myths: The Truth about Teenagers and Reading,*
I tried to speak up for teenagers, and to get adults to question
their assumptions about them. Here the neglected, misunder-
stood, and ignored people for whom I advocate are males who
like to read. As I argue in chapter twelve, "Why Adults Can't
Read Boy Readers," a good part of the reigning belief that boys
don't read is based on the equation of reading with fiction. The
more we value nonfiction, the more likely we are to discover the
intense, intelligent, engaged reading of boys and young men.

Because I am particularly interested in books for teenagers,
the question of how to present nonfiction to my readers inter-
sects with the question of what all books for teenagers set out to
accomplish. I suspect that part of the problem with our books is
that we as adults are overwhelmed. We don't know how to shift
and filter the flood of new information about the past, present,
future, about our genes, our ancestors, and our planet that we
see on the news and in the paper every day. We don't know how
to sort competing theories whose advocates appear on TV stat-
ing cases for and against reparations for slavery, or the rights of
pets, or human cloning. So we don't know what to say to young
readers, outside of dully repeating old ideas, or haplessly trying
to avoid being dull by filling our books with neat factoids and
side bars.

The answer to this dilemma comes, first, in seeing *our* limitations rather than presuming that the problem is the intellectual capacity of our readers—and then in accepting the challenge that YA fiction writers have already faced. In their multivoiced novels they recognize that there are many ways to tell and to understand a story. We have to learn how to give room for readers to think and question with us in our nonfiction books, rather than pretending to an authority we don't have. And yet we must also use our minds to the best of our abilities, reveal our judgments, so that young readers have an example to follow, a whetstone against which to sharpen their wit. Isaiah Berlin's essay is ultimately about history, and the hedgehog approach to that topic leaves room for a lot of individual freedom, but never turns the past into a relativistic mush.

In the essays on nonfiction in this book I urge you my readers to write, publish, review, and circulate books that show more opinion and leave more room for opinion on the part of the reader. I suggest that saying "its all relative" is an avoidance of our adult responsibility to judge, not an enlightened sophistication. I am, once again, asking for standards, as well as for many points of view.

BOOKS IN A TIME OF TROUBLE

In talking about books for younger readers, and especially nonfiction, naysayers often assume that kids will simply not be willing to read a book when they have flashier, more up-to-date, more visually enticing options on screen or online. Our experience as adults overwhelmed by the opposing views we see on TV should show us why that view is wrong. One of the reasons why adults either have snap judgments, or give up and say that coming to a reasoned opinion is impossible is precisely because of watching TV. The masters of the sound bite want to convince you with a quick and easy (well-rehearsed, focus-ground massaged) phrase. Perhaps you will be swayed. But after a few rounds of seeing and hearing these polished performances, you may also give up, seeing all views as some kind of media event.

Books give you the time and place to think. They give you the author and you the reader a chance to weigh, to consider, to balance, and, thus, to arrive at your judgment, your opinion, what you believe to be true. The slowness of books is the gift they offer to us as adults and to young people, who are all the more assaulted and blurred by competing media images. We give young people the chance to actually decide that they do or do not believe in something, that they don't have to react quickly before the next commercial.

The individual and the community, creative freedom and utility, abstract concepts and historical contingencies, particular visions and general truths. These are, I believe, the grand questions that lurk behind our daily online disputes about children's literature. In this book I want to point us to those bigger questions even as we haggle over the smaller ones. An industry so accustomed to talking animals could well spend some time trying to sort out its hedgehogs from its foxes.

Section 1

WHAT IS THE "MULTI" IN MULTICULTURE?

1

✢

Slippery Slopes
and Proliferating Prizes

This essay first appeared in the May/June 2001 issue of the Horn Book. *I originally conceived of it as a dialog with the prominent professor and author Eliza Dresang on the requirement that winners of the Pure Belpré award be Hispanic. Despite many emails, in-person conversations which we transcribed and commented on, and a great deal of effort on both our parts, we could not find a way to turn our differing views into a creative dialog that might be useful for others. One issue she raised, though, led directly to this article: if I disagreed with the ethnic qualification in the Belpré, I had to weigh the principle of ethnic qualification in all awards, including the Coretta Scott King. In retrospect, I am glad that that larger issue came to the foreground. It is interesting, though, that most of the responses to the essay centered on the CSK Award, when, as the title makes clear, it was the extension of the principle of ethnic qualification to the Belpré which impelled me to write.*

I'm sure that nearly every reader of this magazine is in favor of supporting a more diverse children's literature that is in tune with the increasingly multiethnic environment in which we and our children live. I am equally convinced, though, that the American Library Association's (ALA) sponsorship of three awards in which a book's eligibility is determined by the race or ethnicity of its creators is a mistake. For the Coretta Scott King, the Pura Belpré, and the (announced but as yet unnamed) Asian American awards, the creator's biography—ethnic credentials, if you will—predetermines the book's validity. I am convinced that this is wrong. It is the wrong way to bring more kinds of books to more kinds of readers; it is wrong in that it does not evaluate literature in its own terms but by extraneous standards; it is wrong because it is a very slippery slope down which we are already tumbling; and finally it is wrong because even as ALA sponsors more and more such awards, we have not openly discussed and debated their merits. Let's start now.

How can you question the Coretta Scott King Awards, I hear you protesting. Haven't they been a success? Well, yes and no. In one sense the CSK has worked very well. When it was first envisioned by Mabel McKissack, Glyndon Greer, and John Carroll in 1969, no black artist or author had won major recognition from ALA (Arna Bontemps's *Story of the Negro,* a 1949 Newbery Honor book, aside), and there were relatively few African Americans working in the field. Things were not a great deal better by 1982 when ALA recognized the award, although by that time two black authors, Virginia Hamilton and Mildred Taylor, had won the Newbery, and Leo and Diane Dillon (an interracial team) had secured two Caldecotts.

Fast-forward to 2000, eighteen years into ALA's involvement with the CSK, and another African American author, Christopher Paul Curtis, had won the Newbery, while Walter Dean Myers had won the first-ever Michael L. Printz Award for YA books. There is a steadily growing group of African American artists that every important publisher, large and small, seeks to publish. In addition, there are small presses—and even the entire Jump at the Sun imprint at Hyperion—that are devoted to advancing the presence of African American culture in children's books.

Though this rise in African American creators and books cannot be linked solely to the CSK, I do not doubt that the recognition offered by the award, not to mention the passion and enthusiasm of the annual award ceremony, have had positive effects. And in the particular case of African Americans, you could argue that an exclusive award was necessary, especially in the early years. I recall hearing senior publishing people say such things as "blacks don't buy books" or "black books only sell to schools and libraries." In such an environment, it was probably necessary to force publishers, reviewers, and librarians to see how talented black artists and authors were, and to help launch careers that then took off on their own. When combined with Black History Month, the Coretta Scott King Awards created a sales channel that previously had not existed.

For those who have been ignored, denied their due place as creators, as readers, as a public, there is a pure existential value in being acknowledged. There is real power in saying, We are here, we do count, we have something to say. The more frequently and powerfully this point is made, the more new artists are likely to join the field.

But there is an undertow beneath this swell of success. By insisting on testing the racial identity of its winners, the CSK shifts its focus from literature to biography. Who you are, which box or boxes you check on the census form, comes first. Your community, your ethnicity, comes before your talent. And as long as the prize is essentially a community honoring and encouraging its own, it is not clear how the rest of the public is meant to react.

The danger, which to some degree has become the reality, is that this kind of rule balkanizes literature. There is less pressure on the general population to read, understand, appreciate, and develop a fine critical eye for African American literature if a librarian can always think, "I don't have to read those books carefully. The Coretta Scott King Award takes care of that."

An even worse attitude that is all too often the outcome of a balkanized award system is, "I don't have any African American kids in my library, so I don't need to buy books by or about African Americans." As myopic a judgment as that is, the rules for CSK invite it, because they set down a racial standard which others can put to their own uses. If you have to be black to win the award, do you have to be black to appreciate the winning book? The implication that only blacks can write well about blacks sets up the implication that only they can read well about them, too.

The danger in every award that sets limits on the kinds of people, or types of book, that can win it is that it diminishes the pressure on the larger awards, the Newbery and the Caldecott, to live up to their charge to seek the most distinguished children's books of the year.

Speaking as the first winner of the Robert F. Sibert Award for most distinguished informational book for children, I can attest to the mixed effects of receiving a special honor. On the one hand, I was very pleased not only to receive the committee's recognition but also to learn of all of the deserving books that were honored by the Sibert. And yet I could not help feeling sad that the only way we could be noticed was by a kind of admission of failure. It is only because members of the Newbery committees have historically been so averse to nonfiction that we needed the Sibert. Creating a new award is a concession that the other awards will never change.

Advocates of identity-based awards claim that if they select the best of their own literature, the surrounding world will appreciatively buy their selections so that all children grow up learning about all experiences. The problem is that if the award is *from* the community *to* the community, then it is up to the surrounding communities to decide if those experiences—which they are inherently excluded from completely understanding— are vitally important to them. If the award celebrates, instead, individuals who delve deeply into aspects of human experience, no literate, aware reader can afford not to read the books.

We should do everything in our power to encourage the growth of a more diverse literature, but not by predefining who will create it. We should do our best to encourage all readers to be receptive to every brand of literature. Which also means that we must be open to great art, no matter who creates it.

Oddly enough, the CSK committee rules admit this, in a back-handed way. A book is eligible even if only one of the creators is black. What sense does this make? Does the race of one offer a kind of guarantee or validation of the other? That assumes the "authentic" part of the pair has some kind of power over the other, when there is no reason to believe this is so. If this ruling is not about the truth-value of the book, it is strictly a matter of affirmative action: a set number of places are reserved at the table for African Americans, and therefore only they can sit in them.

But here's the trap you get into if you take your stand on affirmative action: you have conceded that you are using identity not as a guarantee of quality but rather to serve a different end; that of advancing the careers of people who may have had difficulty cracking the heedless publishing world. This means that a question of literary deservedness, however softly whispered, will always attach itself to the winners of these awards.

The insistence on ethnic credentials for certain awards has an echo effect on the others. Can any of you who are reading this honestly tell me that if you were sitting in a room with an almost entirely white group of fellow judges (as it would probably be) and a book on a black, or Latino, or Asian American theme by a writer not of that group came up for consideration, you would be willing to select it as a winner? While award committees did this with some regularity in the past (Newberys for *The Slave Dancer* and *Sounder,* for example), the social pressure against doing so increases every time ALA endorses another identity-based award. These awards cause both white writers and writers of color to suffer the imposition of nonliterary criteria on their craft.

Speaking as an editor now, when a manuscript or portfolio comes to me that is related to an experience that I don't know well, I wonder whether the author has it right. And I also think it would be great if I could find a person from a group that is not well represented in publishing to do the art or text for a book that deals with an aspect of his or her culture. That is good sense and good publishing. But that uncertainty should not be codified as a rule someone else sets for me. The challenge is for me to learn enough to determine the value of the text or art myself, to judge it on its merits. And if I have difficulty making that judgment, then it is up to me to grow, to learn, to expand my knowledge.

Expanding the knowledge base of librarians and reviewers is where I think ALA should be turning its efforts. It should focus on diversifying its membership and training its members to appreciate the art and experience of all cultures. The focus should not be on the identity of the creator, which does not tell you anything about the work, but rather on learning how to judge all manner of works on their own terms.

The logic of this position becomes all the clearer when you think about the rules for the Belpré. What does it mean to be Latino? The Belpré rules specify that the winner's heritage must "emanate from any of the Spanish-speaking cultures of the Western Hemisphere." That is somewhere between silly and offensive. For one, it excludes citizens of and émigrés from the largest country in Latin America, Brazil. Brazilians, who are now a major immigrant group in Miami, speak Portuguese, not Spanish. If you include Portuguese-speaking cultures, then New England Cape Verdeans as well as the whole mixed South Asian, black, Amerindian, Chinese, English, Caribbean population—which often has some Portuguese mixed in—are Latinos.

An even more troubling problem this rule poses comes from the role Spanish has played in Latin American history. For indigenous peoples who speak Quechua, or Mayan, or Yanomami, Spanish has been the language of oppression. As these peoples immigrate to America, we are telling them they have to learn the language they resisted in order to celebrate their own culture. If ALA insists on having this rule for the Belpré, it is honor bound to create a new award for indigenous peoples. Otherwise it is in the curious position of supposedly encouraging diversity by rewarding the suppression of native cultures.

The fact that Spanish could be imposed on reluctant peoples points out the most obvious fact about it: it is a language that anyone can learn. It is the very definition of the kind of knowledge an outsider can attain. That is good from my point of view, but it completely undermines the idea that who you are should have anything to do with what you are capable of understanding and creating.

In high school my Spanish teacher, who was Japanese American, introduced me to Neruda, Darío, and, most of all, García Lorca. Reading those poets deepened me and made me understand more about the world. This is what I think awards from ALA should honor: great creators like these poets who, using traditions they deeply understand, add to the imagery, vocabulary, rhythmic pulse, and psychological insight that is our human heritage.

The Spanish requirement is one problem with the Belpré, but the idea of being Latino itself is another. Once you are in, you are in. So an archconservative Miami Cuban could win for writing about being a militant Chicano organizer; an elegant Argentinean émigré could be honored for a novel about being a poor Central American farmer (even though in Latin America that same Argentinean would be the butt of jokes for seeing himself as too European); a member of a family that had lived in the Southwest for hundreds of years could be selected for writing about a Puerto Rican shuttling between New York and Ponce. The umbrella definition of being Latino—which has no precise meaning—allows that person total freedom to deal with any Latino topic, while a person who does not use that term to define him or herself, no matter how knowledgeable about the specific subject he or she writes about, is forever banned from winning the prize. How can a requirement that is both ludicrously capacious and blindly restrictive make any sense?

The worst problem with the Belpré, though, is simply that it was the second ALA prize to include an identity clause in its rules. Two points define a line, which then contains an infinite number of points. Once the principle of identity is confirmed as valid, every group has a right to claim it, as Asian Americans soon did, with their new prize, and indigenous Americans should. Who will bet how soon mixed-race authors, those with disabilities, Muslims (and thus Jews, which, of course, then means Christians), will demand awards of their own? How can ALA say no to any of them? It has abandoned the idea that literature speaks to all and for all and has instead embraced the intellectually passé 1980s Cultural Wars concept that art is defined by a community by its own rules and for its own purposes. Now, any community has a right to demand its announcement, its award, its share of the honor pie.

Fortunately, we have two models that can show us how awards could be handled better. One is an award that honors books entirely based on identity—but not that of the author, only the themes in the books. I am speaking of the Lambda Literary Awards given by the Lambda Literary Foundation for excellence in books about the gay and lesbian experience. The "Lammies" carefully split honorees between gay and lesbian topics, and have many categories reflecting different types of books from young adult through academic. Their literature reflects an acute awareness of the differences among gay, lesbian, bisexual, and transgendered people. Yet nowhere do they specify anything about the sexual orientation, or even gender, of the author. The book wins, no matter who wrote it.

A second model is the award system of the Asian American Writers Workshop. It does pay attention to the ethnicity of the writer, and even has a category of award only for members of the workshop. I think that is perfectly right for them, as an advocacy group. But they are not seeking an imprimatur from ALA. If a librarian reads over their awards list and decides that those are important books, fine. But that is the judgment of the individual librarian, not of a body that represents all librarians, and thus all readers and potential writers, across the country.

The more awards are defined by identity, the less relevant to the world-at-large they seem. I believe that ALA has been hasty in acceding to the demands of fervent advocacy groups without truly opening the issues to debate. So let's have it out. Let's discuss how best to foster the creation, reception, and dissemination of a truly diverse literature.

My suggestion is this: keep the CSK, Belpré, and Asian American Awards, but honor content alone, not identity. Use the very best judges and set the very highest standards for these awards—which may mean that all the winners turn out to be ethnically linked to their topics, but that will be a judgment based on merit, not an *a priori* assumption. Let those committees—who should have a deep knowledge of the cultures and literatures (as well as a knowledge of culture and literature) encompassed by the awards they are judging—struggle with judging a work strictly on its own merits, not its author bio.

I believe this will do even more to foster the best new talent from all groups; it will increase sales of the books, which will no longer be seen as only of interest to one community or another; and it will be intellectually honest. What more can you ask of an award?

2

Awards That Stand on Solid Ground
by *Andrea Davis Pinkney*

The essay reprinted in the last chapter quickly generated a great deal of controversy and discussion, which culminated in the September/October 2001 issue of the Horn Book *with an unprecedented seven pages of overwhelmingly critical letters to the editor. I urge readers of this book who have not read the letters to seek them out on the* Horn Book *website. A number of prominent authors, librarians, and teachers who disagreed with my essay were particularly incensed that it appeared in print without a formal response. The author, editor, publisher Andrea Davis Pinkney gave that reply in the same issue of the* Horn Book. *I print it here so that my readers will have the best chance to weigh and consider all points of view on these issues. In the following chapter I give my response.*

It was with great interest that I read Marc Aronson's article, "Slippery Slopes and Proliferating Prizes," in the May/June 2001 issue of this publication. I appreciate the author's insight into ALA awards, such as the Coretta Scott King Award (CSK) and the Pura Belpré, that celebrate the cultural and ethnic diversities of authors and illustrators. I welcome the author's invitation to debate the validity of these awards. In his piece, Aronson says we have not openly discussed and debated the merits of these prizes. To all interested parties he says, "Let's start now."

So yes, let's begin.

I believe that rather than creating a "slippery slope down which we are tumbling," these awards provide a solid ground upon which authors and illustrators of color and the library and publishing communities can stand. These awards are a gateway to progress. They provide a door for authors and illustrators into the world of children's literature, a world that, despite its increasing diversity, still too often maintains a quiet indifference that is racism in its most subtle form.

Let's start by example. At the urging of my professional colleagues, I recently attended a lecture and slide presentation that was billed as a "comprehensive survey of the history of the picture book." The lecture was given by a noted scholar and children's book publisher, whose survey had a reputation for being the most complete.

I invited an illustrator friend, an African American woman I had recently signed to illustrate a picture book, to attend the lecture with me. She was new to the field. She had illustrated only a few books, two of which I edited.

Of special interest to me was the number of young people in the audience, editorial assistants and junior editors who would someday be acquiring and editing books of their own. (None, by the way, was black.)

The lecture was chronological, moving from the earliest picture books to current ones. I eagerly awaited the section that would cover the 1960s, when African American illustrators such as Tom Feelings, Jerry Pinkney, and John Steptoe came onto the scene.

But there was no mention of them. As the lecture and slide show continued through the seventies, eighties, and nineties, there was still no mention of an African American. The lecture did, of course, highlight the works of Caldecott and Caldecott Honor winners. I was sure John Steptoe's *Mufaro's Beautiful Daughters,* which won a Caldecott Honor in 1988, would be cited. And certainly one of Jerry Pinkney's four Caldecott Honor books would deserve a place on the timeline.

As the lecture concluded with not one single mention of a black illustrator, I felt the acute sense of isolation that comes from unintentional neglect. I felt most saddened for my friend, the new illustrator, and for the young people in the audience, many of whom were not even aware of what they'd missed.

Experiences such as this point to an important truth: a key aspect of awards that hold ethnicity as a criterion for winning is the exposure they afford to black and Latino talent.

Mr. Aronson maintains that these awards are "the wrong way to bring more kinds of books to more kinds of readers." And he says that the receipt of the 2000 Newbery by Christopher Paul Curtis and the receipt of the first-ever Michael L. Printz Award for YA literature by Walter Dean Myers points to progress—all the more reason to do away with awards that celebrate ethnicity, Mr. Aronson's article asserts.

Finally, says Mr. Aronson, in an ideal world editors and awards committees should take it upon themselves "to grow, to learn, [and] to expand [their] knowledge" about other cultures and those authors and illustrators of color who create books about them.

The truth is, we don't live in an ideal world. To my way of thinking, three Newberys (and a handful of Newbery honors) in seventy-nine years does not mark significant progress. I vividly remember the moment it was announced that Christopher Paul Curtis had won the Newbery for *Bud, Not Buddy*. At the awards press conference at the ALA annual midwinter meeting in San Antonio, I, like all of my professional colleagues, eagerly awaited hearing who the year's Newbery recipient would be. When I learned it was Mr. Curtis, I sat on my folding chair and cried.

My tears were a mix of joy and sadness. I was overwhelmed with happiness to know that a black man had received the highest possible honor in children's literature, but then, too, I was saddened by the fact that the last Newbery to be won by an African American was in 1977, when Mildred D. Taylor was recognized for *Roll of Thunder, Hear My Cry*.

In his article, Mr. Aronson makes the point that the Coretta Scott King Award was more necessary in the 1960s when "there were relatively few African Americans working in the field." But there are still only a handful of African Americans in the children's literature arena.

I have worked in publishing for sixteen years. I can count the number of black children's book editors on fewer than my ten black fingers. While there is a growing interest in multiculturalism, many publishing professionals and librarians don't push themselves to expand their knowledge. This is not because they make a conscious choice to ignore other cultures. In my opinion, it is simply a matter of out of sight, out of mind—another example of "unintentional neglect."

Similarly, many young people coming into publishing and librarianship come from predominantly white colleges or communities. Many times they have very limited exposure to people and experiences other than their own. Yet these are the publishers and awards-committee members of tomorrow.

Thank goodness there are awards such as the CSK and Pura Belpré, awards that shine a deserving spotlight on not only some of the best books of the year but the authors and illustrators of color who create them. For some of these young people just coming into the field, this will be as far as they seek to find the works of ethnic authors and illustrators. Fortunately, these awards give them a place to begin. Solid ground on which to stand.

Speaking as a black parent, I, of course, look for books that feature the works of black authors and illustrators. I want to expose my children to the achievements of women and men like themselves. This is true of many other black parents as well.

While I am all for providing my kids with an ethnically diverse home library, I also make a special effort to hold up the important contributions of African Americans. The CSK Award seal lets me and other black parents know instantly that a book has been created by someone who is black. While Newbery- and Caldecott-winning books that have been created by African American authors and illustrators hold a special place on the bookshelves of my children, their scarcity points to the stark ratio of black-to-white winners. When my kids ask why so few books by black people have Newbery and Caldecott Awards stickers on them, I can point them to the CSK Award–winning titles—books that allow children to take pride in black authors and illustrators.

Awards by their very nature are exclusionary. In any awards scenario, when someone wins, someone else "loses," often by virtue of the fact that for reasons of specific awards criteria, they are not eligible to win.

If someone writes or illustrates a stellar work of literature for young people, and that person is not an American citizen or resident, he cannot win the Newbery or Caldecott, no matter how great the book is.

I cannot win the Smarties Book Prize, because I am not a U.K. citizen.

Even though I am American, I cannot become Miss America because I am not between the ages of seventeen and twenty-four. Because I am married. Because I am a mother. And because I am not willing to put on a bathing suit and wear it on television.

To attack ethnic-identity awards solely on the basis of their eligibility requirements only takes the awards at face value. If one digs a little deeper, the merits of these awards become clear. An important aspect of ethnic-identity prizes is that they bring new authors and illustrators into the fold. In 1995, the CSK was expanded to include the New Talent Award (now renamed in honor of John Steptoe). Speaking as a publisher who, almost daily, comes into contact with aspiring authors and illustrators of color who have no point of reference for breaking into the business, I can't say enough about an award that invites and supports newcomers. Thus, ethnic awards offer a wide-open door of opportunity to these bright young talents.

I also speak here as the editor of Sharon Flake, recipient of the CSK/John Steptoe Award for New Talent for her groundbreaking novel *The Skin I'm In,* now in its seventh hardcover printing. I believe that Ms. Flake's talent has been bolstered by her receipt of the Steptoe prize. I believe that Ms. Flake's writing has reached more readers of all races because of the Steptoe award.

The fact of the matter is this: Little is being taken from white writers who cannot receive a CSK or Pura Belpré Award, but denigrating these awards because of their criteria takes something significant from the members of communities who can win these prizes. Attacking these awards insults the creative talents of those who have won these prizes and the committees who work so hard to select the winners for their works.

In his article, Mr. Aronson says, "the more awards are defined by identity, the less relevant to the world-at-large they seem." And, says the article, it would be best to do away with the criteria that requires an author or illustrator to be from a specific ethnic group to win.

I disagree.

These awards are meant to lift up, to inspire. And let us not forget *children,* the true consumers of the books these awards celebrate. To deny young people a means to become exposed to the works of ethnic children's book creators is robbery. Children of color are robbed of the pride they feel in knowing that one of their own has been acknowledged. And white children are robbed of the experience of applauding people other than themselves.

I believe that awards such as the Coretta Scott King and the Pura Belpré are essential to the ALA tapestry. To allow white authors to become eligible for these awards is to turn that tapestry into the monochromatic blanket it used to be.

Andrea Davis Pinkney is an editor at Houghton Mifflin Children's Books and founder of the imprint Jump at the Sun, a line of books celebrating the richness and diversity of black life. She is also the author of Let It Shine: Stories of Black Women Freedom Fighters, *winner of a 2001 Coretta Scott King Honor Award.*

3

Responses to My Critics: The Claims of Principle and of History

The first half of this essay was written before September 11th, it is a good part of what I would have wished to publish as a response to my critics. The second is my more recent review of the issue, nearly a year later.

I would like to thank my colleagues and critics in children's publishing for their thoughtful responses to my essay on slippery slopes. I know many of them personally and their concern to take my objections seriously and to discuss them freely is evident in the letters reprinted in the September 2001 issue of the *Horn Book*, and in Andrea Pinkney's own essay. I have also heard from many authors, artists, critics, and librarians in person and I am grateful for those engaged and sensitive expressions.

I believe I am being fair in summarizing their points of view this way:

> We do not live in a color-blind society, and we do not function in a color-blind publishing system, thus it is either heedlessly idealistic or somehow conspiratorially disingenuous of me to suggest that our awards should be color-blind.
>
> I was overly *optimistic* in claiming success for the Coretta Scott King Awards, since so few African American authors and artists

have won Newberys or Caldecotts; related to this view is a sense that despite the existence of the awards I criticized, and national events such as Black History Month, authors and artists, young readers and concerned adults who are not from dominant groups are still fighting an uphill battle.

I was overly *pessimistic* in not crediting the CSK for the real good it has done, for example in encouraging and supporting several waves of new and talented authors and artists.

To claim that, for example, the CSK awards allow a creator's biography to trump content both slights the criteria used to evaluate books and overlooks the kinds of limitations employed by other awards (nationality for the Newbery, for example).

There is a distinct value in allowing a parent to know in advance that a book has been created by a person who shares race or ethnicity with his or her child.

Lined up this way, it is obvious that while my critics all disagreed with me they were not consistent in their arguments. Thus I could counter the optimists who point to the success of the awards with the pessimism of those who point to lack of award recognition for nondominant authors and artists. Have the awards succeeded or failed? If they have worked, perhaps things are good enough now to allow all creators to compete without predetermining their ethnicity. If the deck is still stacked against nondominant creators, perhaps it is time to consider other approaches. In turn I could respond to those who urge us to confront lingering racism with the happy reports of interracial cooperation on the award committees, and the many careers started and encouraged by the awards.

Winning debating points, though, is not the issue here. Here's the crux of our disagreement: I fear that in seeming to solve the problem of either conscious or inadvertent racism so vividly depicted in Andrea Pinckney's description of the lecture she attended, awards which have ethnic qualifications actually avoid facing it, and thus do not finally achieve their ends. We develop a balkanized literature which, as I said, diminishes pressure on librarians, critics, teachers, parents, and, certainly, editors, to challenge their own insular ideas about the meeting place of children, art, ideas, and books.

Yes, we celebrate authors and artists—and new authors thus get a much better start—but we also create separate strands of literature and experience. I would like to see the American Library Association, the publishing industry, perhaps via the Children's Book Council, all of the review journals, and the schools that teach future teachers and librarians, have workshops in which we raise consciousness, expand minds, and move each and every one of us outside of our limited worldview to open our eyes and ears to other cultures, artistries, and experiences.

With one hand I'd remove ethnic qualifications for all awards, with another I'd insist that our training in children and literature include all children and all literature.

I agree we live in a world afflicted by racism, but I don't think the answer to that is to encourage separate tracks. Rather it is to challenge that point of view in all of us—as those CSK advocates who pointed to and invited multiracial involvement in committee work clearly understood. One librarian I know told me of struggles trying to get books on or by African American authors into a white neighborhood in Staten Island, New York. The books would be trotted out in February, many with CSK labels, then get put away at the end of the month. In turn, I have heard of librarians in Harlem only wanting books on or by African Americans.

Both of these attitudes are wrong and there is no way separate awards can improve the situation. The biased, or self-protective, librarian will always supply minimal compliance. The only way to overcome these attitudes is to force everyone in the creating, publishing, and evaluating system to recognize talent by challenging the comfortable boundaries we place around ourselves.

Those who disagree with me feel the awards have given a toehold in publishing to those who would otherwise have no place: something good is better than nothing. I believe we should not settle for anything less than full integration. The onus must be on all committees, all editors, all publishing houses, all librarians to select the best work, with nothing settled for them in advance. That is why I argued that we should keep the awards we have—CSK for best books on African American themes, individuals, and topics; Pure Belpré for the same with a Hispanic/Latino focus; the Asian American Award, but open up the competition to

all comers. We still recognize the need to support books in these
areas; in the main we will still honor and encourage artists from
the groups the individual awards honor. But we make explicit
our sense that these perspectives are important to all by encouraging all talented people to create such books.

In a personal communication Roger Sutton asked who would
benefit from changing the award rules—would it be only white
people? There is a profound issue here, for I do think there is
perhaps more benefit for whites in the change, but not in the
way his question implied—more awards for white artists and
authors. Rather it is that as a white parent I do feel the need to
integrate the literature my son grows up reading. I do want to be
sure that books are not tracked by race, because that would im-
poverish his experience. Now if my child were completely Asian
rather than mixed, I might be content for him to get more books
on or by Asians, as a counter to a dominant culture. So, yes, I do
believe the need for a truly mixed literature is high among
whites, mainly to ensure that they are not isolated from the rest
of the world. But this is equally true for children in Harlem, who
are impoverished by being exposed to only one strand of human
experience.

To get a sense of the children's book world I have in mind,
think back to that Staten Island community that dutifully dis-
plays CSK books in February but hurries to get them back on the
shelves on the twenty-eighth, and otherwise avoids them all
year. The very kids who are being ghettoized by the attitudes of
adults wear their hats on backwards, listen to rap, and root for
black athletes. Black style, black popular culture, black media
stars are part of their world. That intermixing is the fact of their
lives. But books on black experience are successfully marginal-
ized. I want us as an industry to move past affirmative action to
embrace the mixed world in which we live.

I wrote the above paragraphs before September 11, 2001, and
then stopped, feeling that in the aftermath of the horrible attacks
any kind of dispute on multiculturalism was petty. Returning to
this subject nearly a year later I have modified my thinking
slightly. I can understand that having any award, any prize, even
one whose terms you do not fully embrace, is helpful to a writer.

I can see how both in a sense of arrival and accomplishment, and in sales and thus new opportunities, the awards have been helpful. I also grant that our field has a kind of inertia to it, in which ideas, beliefs about children and the books for them, become entrenched. No wonder it sometimes feels necessary to a group to demand special recognition.

The person who had the greatest effect on my thinking, and most helped to crystallize my sense of what is at stake in this dispute, was Deborah Taylor, Coordinator of School and Library Services at the Enoch Pratt Free Library in Baltimore. She wrote in to the *Horn Book*, and then, much later in the year, we had a chance to discuss and debate the issues in person. I had hoped she could spell out her arguments here, too, but, for a very good reason I will discuss in a moment, she did not think she had the time to do justice to the topic.

Deborah made one very strong point: the CSK has given those who seek a more integrated children's literature, as well as those who simply want there to be more, and more varied, African American voices, a tool that works. As against the powerful currents of racism that define so much of our history, librarians, authors, reviewers, ultimately children, have an instrument, a vehicle, which makes things a bit better.

This is an argument that is fundamentally historical and pragmatic: conditions have been very bad, we have a way to improve them, it works, let's continue it. Deborah is looking into doing a thorough study of prizes with ethnic qualifications to map out exactly how they have worked, what specifically has their influence been on sales, reputations, the growth of new literature. That would be wonderful, much needed, research.

Hearing this cogent argument helped me to define exactly what disturbs me about the ethnic qualifications: for me, this is a matter of principle. Going back to my father's experience in the Pale, I fundamentally cannot accept the idea that we honor, we give value to, we treat as valid, distinctions based on race, or ethnicity, or religion. In other words, while Deborah points to history where these categories have defined human lives, I think of principle, where the categories must be challenged. This is especially true when we talk about art, creativity, creating books that feed knowledge and imagination.

So I have a new compromise to suggest. If the real issue is a matter of pragmatics, if, for example, Deborah's study enables us to define precisely whether and how ethnic awards have increased the number and range of nondominant creators and books, I suggest that we create pragmatic goals. Let us say that when CSK, and Pure Belpré, and any future awards have achieved some specific outcome, we open up the rules to all. Let's establish a monitoring group that will meet in, say, five years to reassess each award and reexamine the rules. That way we do not pretend that we as a community actually support the idea that ethnicity inherently has a place in evaluating books, but we are carefully working out a way to improve our literature. To paraphrase Dr. King, when the first non-African American wins a Coretta Scott King Award we will finally have reached the place where artists are judged not by the color of their skin, but the content of their creations.

I hope my critics will take this suggestion seriously. I hear their pragmatic argument and offer a pragmatic solution. In turn I would urge them to respond to the matter of principle that was actually the main thrust of my essay, and which none of them addressed.

While I agree that the awards have done some good, that the committees are and can be made up of well-meaning judges from many ethnic groups, and that the awards have strict standards not related to race, I do not think they are intellectually justifiable. And the more categories of awards there are, the more sure I am that this is so.

As I should have mentioned in my original essay, Reforma and ALA recognize this without admitting it. They created the Americas Awards that do not have an ethnic qualification, as well as the Pure Belpré that does. If ethnicity is crucial to quality, why have an award that does not make it a consideration? And if you have two different awards with two different standards, why should ALA be allied with the more restrictive, less inclusive one? Switching the rules for the Americas and the Belpré Awards could easily solve this problem.

Which brings me to my final response to my critics. I was frustrated that while many of them wrote eloquently and passionately about individual awards none of them took on the heart of my argument. Each one defended *an* award. None of them engaged with the matter of principle that was reflected in the title of the essay, and throughout the piece: if ethnic groups should have their own awards, which groups qualify? Where do you stop? How do we use the awards to promote the idea that all young readers should be exposed to the best writing and art about all cultures? Since more than a year will have passed between the publication of my initial essay and this response, I hope those who disagree with me will have had time to move away from repeating their original positions to tackling this central problem.

Finally, I felt in some of my critics a kind of shocked anger— "how could you say that?" It was if to question especially the CSK Award was, in another sense, beyond the pale. There was a real pressure to stay silent, not to rock the boat, not to bring up ideas that might challenge beloved awards. It was as if I had betrayed a trust and joined the enemy. I am convinced that part of the emotional force that was directed against me represented a sense, an accurate sense as it turns out, in the supporters of the current ethnic awards that many in the industry silently disagree with them. In other words, beneath the cover of a bland, pallid, liberal support for the awards there is real resistance to them. As I discovered in talking to people who spoke to me privately, making sure no one else knew about it, this is true.

This uneasy balance between supporters who sense hostility that is never directly expressed, and opponents who mutter to themselves and to select friends but say nothing in public is profoundly unhealthy. It is exactly the kind of hidden split under the cover of cooperation that works against real integration. That is why I am all the more convinced it was right of me to publish my essay. If it helped encourage Deborah to do the kind of true historical research this industry needs, it was a great success. The great heart of Jewish tradition is the principle of discussion and debate. And I am glad that, in my particular corner of the literature of younger readers, I have helped to challenge silence, and encourage that ongoing conversation.

Section 2

9/11 AND ITS AFTERMATH, ART

Chapter 4

What Good Is Art, Now?

If the writing year captured in this collection began with debates over culture and multiculturalism, the September 11th attacks quickly changed its character. Like many people I was shaken, and every question about children, literature, art, and society turned back to the tragedy, and how we should respond to it.

What does art have to offer us in a time such as this, a time of tragedy, and fear, a time of war in which our future and that of our children seems so much less certain than it did a month ago? In some way, nothing. No painting, nor poem, nor dance; no novel, nor song, nor sculpture would have stopped the planes from destroying the World Trade Center or the wing of the Pentagon or the jet in Pennsylvania. It is not likely that any art could even have deterred the people who committed those acts. In the wake of such tragedy, art can sometimes seem a frail and frivolous thing, an occupation for a heedless time when nothing else demands our attention. After the Holocaust many thinkers felt art should end, that what had taken place was too absolute, too horrific; there was no room for new creation. The silencing of art would be the only true response. Something like that emotion arises now, a sense that we need to reckon with the real, not the imaginary; the tragedy, not the fantasy.

I think, though, that the weight of the September 11th attacks on our hearts, on our spirit, on our aspirations for our children, actually makes this a very rich and important moment for the arts. So many of us feel we have lost our innocence, our sense of invulnerability. That makes us crave something more real, more solid, more profound than "reality television," or updates on Gary Condit's love life, or the precise details of Mariah Carey's breakdown—all issues that seemed so important on September 10th. We were so preoccupied with the now, the latest toy, the latest show, the latest scandal, the latest megamerger. Now we have more enduring questions about what makes a life meaningful, about the sources of human evil, about how to care for each other well. These are the kinds of questions that artists have addressed for millennia. Art can take us inside of ourselves, past the moment's preoccupations. It is exactly that depth we hunger for now. Two giant buildings can disappear in an instant. What remains as long as human beings live and think and breathe is self-knowledge, and art can help us to find that understanding.

This sounds so grand. What does it have to do with children in schools? Here is where your efforts, and the kinds of activities I'm hearing about from people like you around the country, make so much difference. Bringing poetry, music, theater, painting, dance into the schools is giving young people two gifts that are like those magical presents which appear so often in myths and folktales. They seem like nothing at all, and turn out to be exactly what the hero needs to complete the journey. Teaching young people about art gives them the ability to make something, a magic mirror that reveals more of themselves to themselves than they knew was there, and it gives them a connection to the great art and artists of the past, each of whom created another shard, another fraction of reflecting glass. You make it possible for young people to see themselves and to place those self-portraits in the gallery of self-knowledge.

Though the effects of the arts I'm talking about are profound, that does not mean I'm speaking only about highly serious work. I live on the Upper West Side of Manhattan. On the Friday after the attack we gathered on our street corners and lit candles. Someone mentioned that there was going to be a ceremony at eight o'clock nearby. There is a memorial to fallen firemen near our house on Riverside Drive, though I had never, ever, seen anyone stopping to look at it. At 7:30 we arrived there with our fourteen-month-old son. The space was already filled with people holding candles. A half-hour before the formal event, the crowd was spontaneously singing songs. As we arrived it was "This Land Is Your Land." We joined in on "If I Had a Hammer." I don't have a good voice so I began a very quiet, "We Shall Overcome," that was soon picked up, and passed on, voice to voice, until we all sang it, and "America the Beautiful" and "The Star-Spangled Banner."

There were some Sabbath prayers, and "Amazing Grace," and even "The Battle Hymn of the Republic." But though this was an occasion that touched us all deeply, we did not mainly turn to religion, or war. Instead we returned to the songs we sang in summer camp, in school, the songs of our childhood—which for many of us were the songs of the Civil Rights struggle.

Something as simple as a song you teach a child—a song he or she might make fun of, changing the lyrics into jokes about teachers and school—turns out to be not only one of our deepest sources of comfort, but an inspiration that lasts a lifetime. Singing once again songs that, as children, meant the hope of a better world, and now, at such an imperiled moment, asserted that a world of all peoples all together must endure against even the most vicious attack, linked the decades of our lives, and touched essential chords in who we are. That is what you give a child, when you give a song. I have since learned that prisoners of war during World War II, when deprived of everything else, turned to the songs of their childhood. Now I know why.

With a song you give melody and words that last in a kind of deep memory, to be taken out when we need them. Two gifts. But really you offer much more than that. For as children learn about music and about how to string words together effectively so that they are sweet, or moving, or sad, or inspiring, or witty, they discover their own ability to create, to have that sense of freedom, and accomplishment, and self-reliance that comes from creating on your own. I think this discovery of the capacity to make something, and make it well, is perhaps the most important gift involvement in the arts can give a child, and right now, more and more teachers are recognizing this special power of the arts.

You can see it in the resurgence of poetry for younger readers, which has now been embraced from preschool through high school. Our marketing director at Cricket Books came to us from the Tattered Cover in Denver, perhaps the best independent bookstore in America, where she was in charge of buying books for children. Louise tells me that one of the two most popular promotions they had at the store was "write your own poetry day," when thousands of young people, middle grade and up, came to write, and read, their poetry out loud. The other very popular event was "write your own scary story." Kids want to write.

As teachers have seen and embraced the popularity of poetry, publishers have made more and more of it available, in innovative and attractive forms. From picture books to YA anthologies, from poems celebrating the fifty states to books in English, Spanish, and Spanglish, we are putting poems new and old between covers. This spring, for example, we will publish *Whisper and Shout: Poems to Memorize*. This is a middle grade collection of some old favorites and some very new poems, some limericks and some ballads, some silly rhymes and some serious ones, all selected for young readers to remember and share.

Poetry, or at least an awareness of the rhythm and cadence of crafted phrases, has been entering the schools in another interesting way, through performance and theater. Theater occupies an odd place in the schools. In one sense it is a stalwart. Many schools that have abandoned arts programs, I suspect, still put on class plays, or have drama clubs. And plays are often smuggled into the curriculum as literature—*Julius Caesar, Romeo and Juliet, The Crucible*. And yet it is the rare school that treats theater as an art form whose history and traditions its students need to know. But now theater is cropping up in a new way. Noticing how much young people like to perform and to see performances, people are both turning novels into plays and writing novels meant to be performed. A group in Seattle called Book-It selects a novel, dramatizes it and then stages that play in a regular theater and also in high schools.

In turn some of our best writers for teenagers have begun to liberate the voices in their work from the insistent first person. Virginia Euwer Wolf, a National Book Award winner this year, writes each line as a kind of prose poem, as did Karen Hesse in her Newbery-winning *Out of the Dust*. Walter Dean Myers won the first Michael L. Printz Award—the prize for best book for teenagers—for *Monster*, a book written in the form of a filmscript. We just published *Seek*, by the Newbery-winning Paul Fleischman. *Seek* is a true novel, but written entirely in dialogue and meant to be performed not just on stage, but as a radio play. The very first performance, in Santa Rosa, California, was both live, and live on radio, and the audience included both senior citizens who had grown up on radio plays and the teenagers for whom the novel was written.

Teachers, performance companies, authors have discovered that there are two kinds of power in the written word: its ability to generate images, stories, feelings, sights and sounds within the theater of our own private and individual mind, and its ability to inspire actors, directors, set, costume, and lighting designers to create images for us to see and experience together. This makes sense. Young people grow up in a multisensory, multimedia world: Internet crossed with radio, DVD mixed with school songs, phone calls amidst homework assignments, TV news interspersed with family chatter.

What I find so thrilling about the new interest in performance is that it shows young people that they don't need more technology, they don't need a new player or platform, they don't need cooler headphones, to tap into and respond to their complex world. They can build a performance out of nothing more than their eyes, their minds, and their vocal chords. We are recognizing that the arts empower kids, who otherwise are at the end of a consumer chain where they are simply objects with money. It is like a myth where the hero is the humble person who chooses a simple tool while her greedy or vain or selfish peers grab at apparent prizes that fade into dust. Memorizing a poem or staging a play can seem less glamorous than purchasing a new PlayStation, but one gives the child a gift that can keep expanding without limit, the other requires constantly playing catch-up to a company's marketing strategy.

In 1998 when I published *Art Attack*, it was somewhat odd for me to be writing about abstract art and avant-garde music, such as bebop, for younger readers. There was still a bit of taint in the adult world that made some of the people I was talking about seem so difficult, so incomprehensible, that most adults, much less kids, gave up on getting to know their work. Now, barely three years later, more and more innovative books about painters are being published. Again this matches a new mood. Just as the Art Institute of Chicago has premiered its new show on Van Gogh and Gaugin in Arles, a new picture book about the topic has come out for young readers. Authors are not limiting themselves to popular painters such as Van Gogh. From Chuck Close to Diego Rivera to Jackson Pollack, modern artists are showing up in books for even young children. I think what those publishers and museums are recognizing with their active outreach programs is that many children are drawn to creativity, to innovators who take risks and make us see the world in new ways. Building an appreciation of the arts is not giving kids art history lite, rather it is inspiring them to value creativity, whether in an image of a yellow sunflower, or a powerful mural, a drip painting, or in an idea of their own.

The outreach and audience-building programs that all the major cultural organizations are developing these days are creating new opportunities for us in publishing, and I hope for teachers and parents. For example, the Lyric Opera in Chicago has been eager to do a book that makes their musical form seem less forbidding to young people. We are considering collaborating with them on a book about a twelve-year-old girl who sings in *La Boheme*—an opera whose themes are perfect for teenagers. I am an opera buff, so I was especially pleased to learn of this project from my colleague Judy O'Malley. But what is most significant about it, for you as well as for me, is that it shows how eager arts organizations are to find a way to communicate with young people. We have only begun to explore how to connect museums, symphonies, theaters with authors, illustrators, teachers, and kids. This is a place where you can help us. You are in contact with schools and teachers, and you can help us to learn what they need.

Right now the lead in marrying kids and the arts is coming from individual creators. Chris Raschka has been crafting a brilliant series of books on jazz musicians for very young children and their very appreciative parents: *Charlie Parker Played Be-Bop*, followed by *Mysterious Thelonious*, and, I hear, *Giant Steps*, about John Coltrane. These books are great examples of how the place of the arts in the children's world is changing. Each one is not only about one musician, forming a kind of early picture-book biography, but it is also a unique artwork of its own, so *Charlie Parker* is set to the rhythm of "Night in Tunisia," *Mysterious Thelonious* to "Mysterioso," and *Giant Steps* to, obviously, "Giant Steps." The strangeness of the books is exactly what appeals to children, as I can testify from my own fourteen-month-old son. As I wail and squawk through the bebop sounds, he is delighted, in much the same way as he is when I read to him about the rather magical, surreal, "great green room" in *Goodnight Moon*.

I don't know how many of you remember this, but there is one extremely odd page in *Goodnight Moon*. It is blank, and it reads, simply, "goodnight nobody." Margaret Wise Brown put it there as a kind of blank screen, an entry place for the child's imagination, a break from the cadence of the story where the child could put him or herself. That blank page is what all of you, as advocates for the arts in schools, offer to children. You give them a place to break away from everything we say at them, or define for them, from all of us as quiet old ladies saying hush, where they can create and grow and discover themselves to and for themselves.

But the arts are not merely about self-expression. After all, if you have not mastered your medium, you are limited in what you can say. I remember that in high school I wrote what I thought of as powerful poetry in Spanish, but that was because I only knew rather simple words and grammar, so everything sounded like stripped-down, severe poetry. The arts are also about learning a craft that you can then make your own.

One wonderful example of this is dance. In the sixties we did all those free-form dances, feeling very wild and self-expressive. At a wedding last week I saw an older couple do a fox-trot, and it looked wonderful. The containment of the form they had mastered allowed them to go past what they might have done on the spur of the moment, and to test their capacity for rhythm and movement. The choreographer Bill T. Jones created a marvelous picture book for young readers with the photographer Susan Kuklin called, simply, *Dance*. In its lavish pages you can see the freedom of movement a trained body has achieved.

Just now I am working with Susan, and Chris Raschka, to plan out a book around a classical ballet instructor. Elena Tchernickova, who trained the dancers at American Ballet Theater for many years, is working with a very talented thirteen-year-old. We will try to capture the transmission of culture as Elena shapes a role on the body of this young girl.

As Elena explains it, each subtle hand movement, each slight difference in the arc of a back or extension of a leg, in a classical ballet contains social history—hearkening back to the courts of Louis XIV, Louis Napoleon, and the Romanov tsars—artistic history—as she describes how a lineal succession of great dancers performed that very step, and made it their own, and personal history—as the girl must find in herself the wellsprings of the emotion the character is depicting. Bringing the arts into the schools, then, is not just allowing young people to experience, develop, or even to appreciate an art form. It gives them an entry point into our history and into themselves. The emotions and ideas poets, playwrights, actors, painters, dancers have captured are what we all experience, what young people are starting to see in themselves. As you give them the gift of the arts, you give them the capacity to see into themselves, to recognize in their internal experiences a link to our collective past, our collective self-understanding.

Elena's linking of ballet to social history is an important track that I hope more people use in the schools. The history of artistic creation is also the history of a time and place. In 2004 there will be a major celebration of the hundredth anniversary of the death of Anton Dvorak. The music critic and historian Joseph Horowitz is organizing a nationwide effort, linking orchestras—including one here in New Jersey—with schools. Their focus will be the story of Dvorak's New World Symphony, the piece he created to establish an American music. As it turns out, Dvorak worked closely with Henry Burleigh, an African American singer, and he consciously and deliberately made his American music one that drew on the tunes, melodies, and sounds of many kinds of Americans. Inside a piece of classical music is the story of multicultural America. I hope to have the chance to work with many of you as 2004 grows closer, because I think this is a very exciting project.

The arts always face something of a battle in the schools: fights over funds and time, disputes over practicality and utility, flare-ups over morality and appropriateness. I cannot promise you that any of these will go away. In fact in a tightening economy they may only increase. But I think that the hunger for more depth, more truth, even for a style of humor and diversion and romance that entertains us but does not insult us, is our ally. The shift back to the arts in schools that was well on its way on September 10th, became all the more vital the following day. Something essential in ourselves, our way of life, our hope for the future has been challenged. And as we search for a solid core to hold onto and to pass on, there the arts stand offering young people a way to grow and to appreciate what human beings are capable of creating. We offer them a mirror, a blank page, and thousands of years of history in how to use them. In a time of destruction, what better gift could we possibly give?

Chapter 5

Of Camels
and Needles' Eyes:
Art and Young Readers

I was invited to host a day dedicated to the arts and children at an International Reading Association convention. While the IRA in general is aimed at children younger than teenagers, and the other presenters with whom I spoke, and who are mentioned here, write and illustrate for those readers, this is really an extension of the talk I gave about the arts after 9/11. Because all young readers are embedded in some kind of educational environment, at home, in school, or both, the question relates to all ages of how art, which can seem to encourage the individualistic and the untamed, fits with education, which, at least in part, has to do with the transmission of skills, received ideas, and established values.

Welcome everyone to a day dedicated to the arts, to young readers, and to the connections between the two. It is astonishingly appropriate to me personally that we should be gathered here, in San Francisco, to spend this day together. My aunt, Trude Guermonprez, lived here, and she was an accomplished weaver, as did my grandmother, Johanna Jalowetz, a bookbinder and singing teacher. They came here from Black Mountain College where my grandfather had taught music. At that school, which, since its demise, has become quite famous for the experimental art that it encouraged and developed, my grandparents became friends with a young couple. She was a Japanese American who had been housed in the internment camp at the Santa Anita racetrack during World War II. Among the other detainees were three animators from the Walt Disney Studios. They encouraged Ruth Asawa to draw, and she did, hour after hour, every day. She kept on making art in college. Albert Lanier, her future husband was interested in architecture.

Ruth and Albert eventually moved here to San Francisco, where she devoted her life to her sculpture—you can see some of her famous pieces in public spaces such as at the fountain near Union Square—and, especially, to bringing arts into the schools. Ruth is remarkable for having done throughout her life what she had to do in the camp, find a way to make art that engaged with history, that faced difficulty, but also that celebrated life. When her children were born she did not choose between art and education, she brought art into education, as something all could share. Long before she met me, my wife came here to join in that effort with Ruth, so we both knew her before we knew each other. Ruth is still active—a retrospective of her work will be shown at the Oakland Museum from June 15 to September 22—but she could not be with us today. I would like, then, to present Addie Lanier, Ruth and Albert's daughter, and a high school teacher, with this Reading Excellence through the Arts award. Ruth Asawa lives the arts in education, which is more inspiring, perhaps, then anything else we can say today.

Having honored Ruth it is only fair that I let her speak first. She has said, "Art teaches discipline. Craft. Respect for tools and for sharing. And finally, self-respect. Where else can you teach all that at once?" Let's look at what art does, and how it does it, and what that allows you to teach.

Art, artists, young people, reading—how do these related but also quite different entities fit together? In one sense there is a simple and direct line: an artist creates, a young person reads a book to learn about the creator and his or her art. But in reality the transmission belt, the sequencing, is much more interesting and more fraught. Art occurs at the intersection point of two very different forces, and the dialogue, the dialectic, between them runs through this entire process. On the one hand, as Ruth says, art requires training, discipline, craft. On the other, it is a product of invention, innovation, inspiration. It is the extension of skills the artist has acquired, and it is a new creation that establishes a new set of rules around itself. Art, then, is very like reading—a skill one must master, which then leads in countless unbounded directions.

The primary challenge is communicating to young readers both aspects of art, the wild and the tame. For the moment I'm going to call that first problem the black swan or the white. You'll see why in a few minutes. Challenge two might be called the camel and the needle. All art takes place in three dimensions. That is most obvious for the performing arts—dance, theater, live music—but it is equally true for painting and sculpture. When any of us attends a performance, or goes to a museum, or listens to a recording we experience the moment sensually. We are taken out of our daily life and immersed in something else. A book does not necessarily have that power. It is one object amidst many: we see past the borders of the page to our piled-up desks; no matter how quiet the library we hear the world around us; when we read about a dancer, we are not in a hushed theater seeing her pirouette across the stage.

The great challenge that the creators you will hear from today have faced is how to make the book so captivating that it too becomes a kind of performance, it too enraptures you, it too removes you from your surroundings and takes you into another kind of space. The camel must pass through the needle's eye of the two-dimensional book so that it can enter a kind of heaven. That blessed place is where the reader, the young person, sees, hears, understands the world in a new way, where something new, a new sense of art has been added to his or her life.

But the challenges do not end there. Having gotten past the black swans and white ones, camels and needles, you teachers reach the third act where the process begins all over again. I'd call that, "a thousand flowers bloom." If the difficult task the author must face is capturing three-dimensional art on two-dimensional paper, the opportunity you as teachers have is to turn the book back into some kind of physical event. If readers are inspired by a book on art to try out their own hands, feet, vocal chords then they become not just appreciators of art, but nascent creators.

This is the great compensating advantage books on art have. They can go beyond transmitting information about existing artists to inspiring a new generation to find their own artistic impulses. The baton is passed, and art busts out all over. And yet, as I said at the start, art is only half about inspiration; it is equally about training. So your challenge is to channel the energy the book releases, so that kids are not just splashing around in their own impulses, but are taking the first steps towards harnessing them, towards making something in the world, towards being artists themselves. As you may recall, it was shortly after Mao encouraged the many flowers to bloom that he stomped them out.

Let's see how each of these challenges affects you. In a sense a child and an artist are mirror images of each other. Ever since the end of the nineteenth century, artists have sought to tap their own unfettered, childlike, open-ended sensibilities. They want to become less rule-bound so they can create art that is as new and interesting as science, technology, social change. This trend is what I wrote about in my book *Art Attack*. It is as if, having spent a lifetime covering over a white board with black paint, they seek ways to scratch away that covering to find the white space beneath it. Children are going in the opposite direction. They need training not only to enter the adult world, the common world all around them, but even to recognize and identify the creative forces within themselves. You don't know you like to play music until you get a drum or recorder or keyboard and learn how. They want to fill the white space with black lines.

The seemingly opposite missions of artists and children present, I suspect, something of a problem for teachers. Those who are tepid or skeptical about using art with young people have had their fill of zany artists and think of art as a kind of lazy diversion, a soft-focus activity that encourages kids to "be creative" when they would better spend their time acquiring skills; or they see art fans as given to a flaccid and patronizing judgment that "appreciates" every pot holder, ashtray, finger painting a child makes just as they nod approvingly at every loony, slapdash effusion of modern art.

Art, to these critics, seems just the opposite of education. That is because they are equating art entirely with the creative side of our initial duality of wild and tame. They miss the very meaning of the word "art," which has its root in the Greek word for skill or craft. Think of the other uses of the term: the art of war, the art of persuasion, the art of diplomacy.

Still, they are onto something. It is all too easy to think of art as a kind of unsupervised gym class in which kids run around and have fun, and your job is to make sure that they do not create too much mayhem. Here is where books about the arts have something extraordinary to offer, for they take us into the work, the labor, the investment of time and sensibility involved, for both the artist and for the person who has created the book. I would urge you to bring young people's attention not just to art as expression but as creation, not just inception but formation, not just inspiration but cultivation. Art, after all, is ultimately about selection, it is about what you remove from the rest of life to highlight as a comment, a counter, a mirror, a reaction, to that life.

In Chris Raschka's *Mysterious Thelonious* he quotes Thelonious Monk as saying, "there are no wrong notes." To which I would answer, that is true, if you are Mr. Monk. If your sensibilities and sensitivities are that refined, yes. And, yes, even as you start out, at the very beginning when you are just feeling your way. But after that, there are acres and acres of wrong notes that you have to discard to find the right ones to play.

Let me give you an example of what I mean. Elena Tchernickova is a woman who has devoted her life to classical ballet, as a dancer, as a ballet mistress for major companies around the world, and now as a teacher of young people. I have been trying to develop a book that passes on some of that accumulated wisdom to a broader audience. I want you to hear what Elena has to say about one moment in one ballet. I think you will immediately recognize that what she is discussing is the opposite of fuzzy effusion. And yet, oddly enough, she is discussing a moment in a ballet that is precisely about the balance of existing rules and new innovation that I've been talking about. I am quoting from her words, as I transcribed and lightly edited them.

Swan Lake, which premiered in its modern version towards the very end of the nineteenth century, in 1895, was choreographed by two different men. A newcomer named Lev Ivanov did the second and fourth acts, which feature the white swan. Ivanov was influenced by a new focus on feelings and impressions in the arts. He did not just want to put a dancer through her standard positions, but also wanted her to create the feeling of a character on stage.

The first act, which sets the stage for the ballet, and the third, the black swan's act, were choreographed by Marius Petipa, who had trained Ivanov. He was the essence of tradition, the old school. The *Swan Lake* we see is not exactly what these two men created. The American dancer Isadora Duncan created pieces that were completely about her emotion and her body. When the choreographer Michel Fokine saw her work, he was amazed, transfixed. When he invented the solo of the dying swan, he based some of her gestures on Isadora's emotionalism. As ballerinas saw Fokine's swan, they began to change their parts in *Swan Lake*. By the early twentieth century, there was a huge difference between the white and the black swan acts in *Swan Lake*.

The white swan uses classical steps such as the pirouette and the arabesque, but in a new, looser way. In the second act, when the white swan tells the prince her sad story, that she is half a swan and half a human being, she looks down at her reflection in the water of the lake. She is gazing at herself to see how human she is and how much still a swan. She must be completely *in* her role. And when she begins to move, she breaks the rules.

Even though we see the standard positions of classical ballet, we are not just seeing a ballerina doing perfect steps, we are seeing a character who molds, who transforms, those steps to become a bird, a creature of flight. The white swan's part is not just a series of positions, it is an impression, an image of a magnificent pure white bird that is also human.

In the third act, the black swan is colder, more calculating, and her steps are pure classical, like a ballerina from an earlier age. When she moves, spins, pirouettes, her steps are precise and exactly by the rules. There are just two moments when she stops being the cold, perfect classical dancer. As she moves across the stage in a diagonal, trying to convince the prince that she is actually the white swan, she notices that he seems upset. When she sees that, she loosens her arms, she starts to play the white swan. She is like a thief, using the magic that makes people not notice him; she changes her face. In an instant, she becomes the white swan, he doesn't see the transformation, but we do.

The only times in the whole ballet when the black swan breaks the classical rules are those two moments when she fears the prince can see through her, and so she must become the white swan. The black swan cannot give us the feeling of flight that the white swan offers, but she can imitate that softness just enough to fool the prince. In those two moments in the black swan's dance before the prince, ballet shifts from following rules to being a kind of visual poem.

What I hope Elena and I can do in the book is to get young readers to see just that one instant, that moment, where a dancer's artistry, her craft, allows her to be a black swan imitating a white swan, while spinning across the stage. If we succeed in doing that we have done much more than make them into ballet fans, into art appreciators. Instead we will have given them a sense, a hint, of what art can do: revealing by concealing, exposing by disguising, telling the truth by acting. And all of that is about technique, not free play. We will have given them an entry into the true magic of art, which is not to express but to create.

One reason we like creating and publishing books about art for young people, and, I assume, why you like having them, is that they are lively, colorful, enjoyable—in a word, fun. It is cool to see nice color images of an impressionist painting, or a trained dancer, or pastel evocations of a piece of music. You may be able to entice a nonreader, or a poor reader, to pick up an art book simply because it is attractive, or unusual. In other words, the creator of the book has succeeded in passing on a bit of the magic, the charge, of the live event through the medium of the page.

But just as concentrating on the white swan side of art—the impressionistic, free-form, innovative aspect—misses the black swan—the training, rules, calculation—so using an art book to entertain a child misses the much larger opportunity you have. Art awareness, art knowledge, is a kind of literacy just as decoding letters and understanding words is. It is a conduit to, as Mathew Arnold put it, "the best that has been thought and said." We tend to shy away from phrases like that these days, not wanting to seem to have cultural prejudices, to favor one art over another. But this seeming generosity is actually a kind of miserliness. We are refusing to extend to young people the accumulated wealth of creation and accomplishment that is their birthright. If we do not give young people entry to this cultural legacy we are hoarding it for ourselves.

It is exactly as if you as teachers refused to teach vowels because that might be deemed prejudicial to consonants, and kept your students on a steady diet of tongue-twisting Slavic names. You would watch them choking and have to claim that it was good for them. I do think young people are choking for lack of access to the arts, and while you cannot remedy this societal issue, you can relieve their misery. You can feed them books filled with art not merely as a kind of visual candy, but as an appetizer to an extended meal that you are inviting them to participate in and enjoy.

Well, how do you do this? How do you join with the creators of books to pull the genie out of the bottle, drag the camel through the needle, bring the arts through the pages of the book alive and kicking into your classrooms? While each of the authors and artists here can speak for him or herself, this is what I suggest you listen for and think about.

Chris Raschka's trilogy of jazz books, *Charlie Parker Played Be-Bop*; *Mysterious Thelonious*; and *Giant Steps* are both reading experiences and performances. That is, they reflect actual performed music, and they can also be performed when read. Each book offers you as a teacher a chance to have your students listen to the original music, and to the rhythm and music of the text, and to make connections between the two. You can literally embody the books by following the word patterns, the color schemes, the cues Chris has given you. You might then ask young people to write something that echoes a piece of music they know, not as lyrics, but as a sound portrait, or visual image. Just as Chris invites them to bring the music alive again with his books, you can challenge them to capture a genie, the sounds in their lives, and trap them in a bottle of their own devising.

Patrice Vecchione's *Whisper and Shout* offers a second kind of artistic transformation. As you will see, when we meet the fifth graders she is bringing with her, she has selected poems by other authors that are particularly suited for young readers to memorize and to perform. We will see and hear for ourselves how well they take to that two-step challenge: first bringing a poem into their minds and mouths and bodies, and then giving it back to others as their own transformed possession, to display and to share.

Paul Fleischman could not be here today, but he was the first one to make the case to me of the importance of memorizing. As he put it, a poem you know by heart is like anything else you own, you can look at it in private, examine it, share it, use it as a bridge to others. It becomes a cornerstone of your own inner and personal library. Patrice will give us a chance to see that library in use.

Susan Kuklin's books *Dance, Harlem Nutcracker,* and *Swoops* offer two kinds of artistic journeys. On her pages she has captured bodies in motion. She invites young readers to experience the physical vocabulary of motion with her large, clear, sculptural images. Like Elena, she makes you see a moment that in life would just rush past and capture in your eye all of the grace, the lyricism, the training, the wit that a dancer's body reveals in that instant. Students are invited to embody them by testing their own abilities to move and shape their limbs in space. But if you are paying attention, her books are doing something else, they are showing how an artist's eye works with a camera. In other words, the books are not just about what the camera sees and captures, but about the camera itself. You can invite students to think about how they would try to capture motion in stillness.

Judd Winick's memoir in the form of a graphic novel reveals yet another way image and text can marry in telling a story. For your students who are growing up amidst constant visual stimulation, I think Judd opens a very exciting prospect: how do you describe your life in words and images together, how do you shape the images to tell the story? When do you slow down, and when do you fast forward, when do you go in tight with a close-up and when do you pan back to take in the whole scene? Then, how do you select words to be the right counterpoint to this visual display? Kids who watch videos and spend hours on PlayStation games know very well that word and text together tell stories in very interesting ways; why not harness that knowledge to get young people to tell their own? This in no way asks less of words. As any of you who have read *Pedro and Me* know, the marvel of the book is not that Judd let the picture tell the story or skimped on words, but rather that he did an excellent job, really a poet's job, of picking just the right ones.

Finally in Stephen Kroll's *Ellis Island* we see how a creative class and teacher can evoke an entire world, a moment in history out of a book, bringing it alive in the classroom.

Art is out in the world in three dimensions. The creators you will meet today, and many like them, try to capture that lived vitality in two dimensions. They give you the treat of a book that has many real and potential dimensions. You have words and images. You have the potential to embody text and art, in sound, in performance, in motion, in new combinations of art and text that your students create themselves. And, finally, books about the arts lead into the arts; they are, you might say, individual yellow bricks that hint of a much wider and more magical road just ahead.

This year we at Carus are publishing our first nonfiction book; appropriately it is about how the arts of the lands of the Silk Road have been continued and transformed here in America. I encourage you to think of this whole day as an invitation to join in the caravan of the arts, as teachers, as creators, as fellow travelers. It should be a lively trip.

Section 3

9/11 AND ITS AFTERMATH, HISTORY

Chapter 6

Puritans and
Fundamentalists,
a Prolegomena

I wrote and edited a good part of this piece while on the train to make the speech reprinted in chapter four. Whether it was art, culture, or history, I was urgently seeking some grounding to make sense of the world at large, and my profession in children's books in the wake of the terrorist attacks. I was especially grateful to Luann Toth of School Library Journal *for managing to get it into print so shortly after I wrote it, when so many of us were searching for some larger context for our experiences.*

I had just finished writing a book called *Witch-Hunt: Mysteries of the Salem Witch Trials* (Atheneum, 2003), when the September 11th terrorist attacks took place. For months I had been immersed in the testimonies of accused witches and their "afflicted" accusers, as well as modern studies that tried to make sense of their seventeenth-century beliefs. Day after day as I read statements from Islamic extremists and defenders of the West, they reminded me of the world I had just finished studying and describing. One reason I had wanted to write about the trials was to render a more complex and sympathetic portrait of the Puritans, including their leaders such as Cotton and Increase Mather. That dark period in our own history offers lessons for both America and its enemies today.

The word Puritan has come to have a negative meaning in America, suggesting repressed and repressive people who use religion to stamp out any signs of life in society and themselves. No event is more emblematic of that reading of the Puritans than the Salem witch trials, which resulted in the hanging of nineteen people and a total of twenty-five deaths (one person was crushed by having rocks heaped on his chest because he would not make a plea—which was standard practice at the time. Five died in prison). Yet how would those same devout people appear to us if we employed the other term often used for them in England, the Godly? They might remind us of the fundamentalists Osama bin Laden has called to arms, in a struggle of the faithful against the unbelieving. But that very association complicates the picture: we are fighting against our own past, and he is articulating a deep yearning for faith and community that runs through all of our history.

When the English gave the name Salem, or peace, to a place the Wampanougs called Naumkeag, they made a solemn covenant with "the Lord and one with an other; and do bind ourselves in the presence of God, to walk together in all his ways." Here was a community in which social and religious bonds were united. This appealing ideal was meant both to blunt the edges of any individual's difficulties in the world (for example, just prices were set so that no one could take advantage of another's need) and to fulfill a sense of spiritual destiny. By limiting their congregations to the truly saved, and building their communities around those churches, the Puritans believed they tied the fate of their settlements to God's grand design. Today we often hear how extremist groups, such as Hammas, fulfill many social needs that the government is unable to meet, providing schools, clothing, food, shelter for the poor. In addition, like the Godly of Salem, the modern radicals offer the assurance that their transcendent religious truth will soon triumph over any current secular rulers.

These parallels between American beliefs in the seventeenth century and the beliefs some fundamentalists hold today are not merely a historical curiosity. On the one hand, the spirit behind Salem, the effort to build communities around social sharing and deep faith, runs through all of our history—among many traditional Indian peoples, in the Shakers, the Mormons, the Lubavitchers, the Southern Baptists in both black and white forms, and innumerable other congregations. On the other hand, the passage from Salem's foundation in commitment and hope in 1629 through the witch trials in 1692, points to what may be a hopeful direction for those sincere believers around the world who were sickened by the terrorist attacks.

Historians debate what caused the accusations of witchcraft in Salem and why the courts disregarded their previous laws of evidence and trusted in the rabid courtroom fits of the accusers. Certainly local ministers such as Samuel Parris supported and egged on the accusers, who, in turn, used the language of religion in their indictments of supposed witches. But religious belief played a much more complex role in the trials. Leading ministers such as Cotton Mather, and, especially, his father Increase—arguably the moral leader of the colony—raised many questions about the trials. More importantly, perhaps, it was individual Puritans, taking the strictures of their religion very seriously, whose conscience-struck recantations broke through the hysteria of the courtroom scenes.

The true believers found that they could not lie, even when telling the truth would cost them their lives. Margaret Jacobs visited the cell of a man who would hang the next day, in part due to her testimony, and admitted she had done wrong. "I was in such horror of conscience that I could not sleep for fear the Devil should carry me away for telling such horrid lies." It was the voices of people like Margaret that made more and more people doubt the trials. In a wrenching choice between the judgment of the community, which was that the Devil himself was loose in their midst, and of their own individual consciences, an ever-increasing number of devout Puritans took the harder path. God as they heard that voice inside spoke louder than God as the ever more whipped up anger and vengeance of their neighbors, family, and friends.

Increase Mather articulated this personal voice of doubt into the principle that effectively stopped the trials: "It were better," he wrote, "that ten suspected witches should escape, than that one innocent person should be condemned." Ironically, it was in the courage of dissenting individuals that the community of faith found its greatest expression. This did threaten their group cohesion, and the nation their descendants helped bring to birth in 1776 was secular, not religious. But it was one in which conscience, whether in the form of abolitionism, or women's rights, or environmental activism, or concern for the rights and freedoms of Arab Americans, could never be silenced.

The lesson of Salem for secular America is that the rhetoric of our current enemies expresses the most fervent yearnings of our ancestors. Devout Muslims may take a different but equally powerful lesson from the trials. It took individuals of courage to question false rumors and malicious accusations then, and the same is true now. The more individualistic Westerners understand the hunger for a community of faith, and the more believers who mimic the phrases of their leaders question their own hearts, the sooner this trial will end.

Chapter 7

Puritans and Fundamentalists, an Exploration

Shortly after the previous piece was published in School Library Journal, *Professor Gary Sick, who is married to the well-known New York City librarian Karlan Sick, asked if I would be willing to discuss and explore the ideas I had sketched out in an afternoon brown-bag seminar at Columbia University. Professor Sick runs the Middle East program there, and thought it might be an interesting discussion. Feeling some trepidation because I am not a scholar of Islam or the Middle East, I accepted and wrote the following talk.*

The tone of the talk is unlike anything I would use in addressing younger readers, but as it happens many of the ideas in it came to me while researching my book The Land of Promise *(Clarion, 2004), which is the second book in my trilogy on the colonial period. In a sense the talk, and the book, are my effort to put into practice what I ask for in the first essays on the prizes. I think all of our histories matter to all of us, and a true multiculturalism arises not primarily from respecting separate traditions as if they were a kind of capital owned by an ethnic group but by studying all groups and finding the surprising links and crosscurrents among peoples.*

Many discussions of the conflict between certain Islamic groups and the United States, or more generally the West, refer to those groups as "puritan." And while the authors use the term in the lower case without a specific historical resonance, there are elements of some contemporary Islamic ideas that are reminiscent of a certain brand of seventeenth-century Protestantism: the focus on purity of faith and practice; the idea of returning to a supposedly unsullied form of the faith in rejection of its intervening adaptations; a sense of being involved in an ultimate struggle against a force that is evil incarnate; the centrality of the idea of the exile and Promised Land, as place and as metaphor; even the particular intensity of the emphasis on women acting in a prescribed fashion, including modest dress. I hope that looking at the crosscurrents in some of those ideas in their earlier versions might open up new questions about their current form.

A couple of years ago, Salman Rusdhie wrote a novel called *The Ground beneath Her Feet*. In a sense that is my theme. The seventeenth-century Puritans felt the ground shifting beneath their feet. Consulting their sacred text, they discovered the true meaning of the seismic rumbles and labored to speed along the great transformation they divined was coming, and yet they also experienced change as something imposed from the outside, by their enemies, and they fought fiercely to resist it and return to an earlier way of living. Looking back at their moment, they were right to feel the rumblings, the shifting, the sense of peril and promise. It is just that the language they had available, or chose to use, is not the one we would use now. The question that poses for us today is what similar deep shifts Islamic fundamentalists are registering, and where that may point for the future.

As many of you know, the name Puritan was a pejorative term applied to people who called themselves the Godly, or considered themselves to be seekers. But it captured something about these Calvinists in England and later New England: they did want to purify the Protestantism of their day and return to the faith and practice of the original Christianity in the time of Jesus. They wanted to rid their faith of the impurities that had crept into it in the long Catholic night, and the more recent vacillations of the Church of England.

The Godly believed they had the opportunity, the necessity, to live the real Christianity as it had not been practiced for 1600 years. In John Foxe's extremely influential *Book of Martyrs*—which, incidentally also advocated martyrdom for the cause of faith—he gave his version of the history of true religion, based on his reading of the Book of Revelations. As he saw it, Christianity had passed through four previous phases: the original and pure church that was persecuted by the Romans; the mingled church after Constantine when it merged with the Roman Empire; the phase from the fall of Rome through the Norman Conquest, when the papacy subverted the truth; and the reign of the Antichrist, which began when Gregory VII became pope in 1073. The fifth and final period began with the Reformation. This chronology meant that the Puritans were precisely at the end and beginning of time.

The Puritans believed that the final battle with the forces of the Antichrist was about to begin. They could see the face of this ultimate enemy in the Whore of Babylon, the Catholic Church, which had stolen the faith. The Antichrist was often seen as the papacy, but could also be seen as the Church of England's Archbishop Laud, or the Catholic circle around Charles I, or Catholic rulers in Europe, or even, Protestant ministers who were not truly saved. Fighting this last battle would be followed by a chiliad or millennium, a thousand year reign, of the saved, the elect, the saints. This would take place here, on earth, and very soon.

Fight without mercy because the enemy is evil itself; live as saints, for the rule of the saved is about to begin—these are the charges the Puritans experienced from their moment in time. This is why they were so resistant to compromise and so fervent about matters of doctrine and practice. If not merely your personal fate but the entire meaning and course of human history is being judged, it is crucial that pagan images be stripped from churches, that no sports be allowed on the Sabbath, and that, as Roger Williams insisted, women only appear in church wearing veils.

But why, one might ask, did they experience the world this way? Why did a growing minority of people in England and something close to a majority of the 20,000 or so people who came to New England between 1630 and 1640 see their own time as the end of all time?

Here is where space comes into the picture. In England, this kind of thinking started out as a defensive mode. It expressed the sense of militancy and peril felt by Calvinists who thought that the reformation of their faith that began with Henry VIII had not gone far enough. By the time of Charles I, they thought pure religion was in danger of being entirely suppressed by the king and his evil archbishop. This sense of threat in England was not merely about how the Godly could worship, it also expressed a belief that England was avoiding its obligations to fight the world Catholic menace and was in grave danger of drawing down on itself the wrath of God. England was being tested and found wanting.

The New World, the Land of Promise, as the great Puritan minister John Cotton called it, was another matter. In one sense it was a place of exile, a wilderness into which the faithful could escape. The narrative, in that sense, shifted from the Book of Revelations to Exodus. But in another, the sense of promise implied a hope both for material success and for ultimate redemption. This land seemed to have been emptied of its prior inhabitants, or filled with the missing lost ten tribes of Israel, just so it could be the place on which the last stages of history could be enacted.

Psychologically, then, the sense of being at the end of time was both a feeling of great peril and of exceptional, even unique promise, and where you were physically gave one or the other interpretation to your worldview. A question I have for the Islamicists here is about how space plays out today, the differences between Wahabism expressed as a dominant view in Saudi Arabia and what is often called Islamic fundamentalism as an insurgent or revolutionary view elsewhere. I realize that the two psychological and physical territories were not entirely separated in the seventeenth century, and interact all the more today. Still the balance of promise and peril has something to do with how much in the majority or minority you feel you are.

What were the broader, or nondoctrinal, reasons for the Puritans' binary, apocalyptical, thinking? One interesting suggestion, that again seems quite contemporary, is the availability of Bibles and other religious materials in print in English. By 1640, over one millions Bibles had been printed in England. More and more individuals could read, and, they now had access to the book that explained everything. As one Puritan preacher put it, there is "no part of true philosophy, no art of account, no kind of science rightly so called, but the Scripture must contain it." Many of those readers attempted to puzzle out the Great Book's hidden meanings, and passionately resisted having a bishop or other leader tell them how to interpret it. The explosion of access to the Bible insured that more and more people would interpret their experiences within the frame of biblical stories and predictions, without any outer guidance. The potential parallel to today is how various forms of modern technology, especially those that cannot be controlled centrally, lead to the proliferation of seemingly antimodern religious ideas. Radio and the Internet are the first two that come to mind.

The irony in the case of the seventeenth century is that the very proliferation of biblical interpretations and prophecies eventually led to a skepticism about the Bible. Reading, and the Bible in English, which seemed to offer the great chance for salvation, instead led some to place reason ahead of any deity, or to question the absolute truth of the Bible. Precisely because the Bible was thought to be the means of final salvation and its meaning single and clear, conflicts of interpretation ultimately led some thinkers to question its authority.

This emphasis on reading worked out in a particularly interesting way for girls and women in New England. While a girl was reared to be a good woman who "governed her tongue" and respected the authority of her husband and the male leaders of her community, she was taught to read. Female reading did, as ministers feared, lead to reading novels, developing a personal, inner fantasy life, and then writing letters, diaries, and even novels that expanded that inner space. The Islamic schools are much in the press these days. I wonder if anyone has studied not just what the students are taught, but the extent to which pupils absorb, reject, debate those texts and ideas. It seems to me the effects of teaching should be evaluated not on what the school and teacher profess but on the meanings the students make.

The question of the social and economic causes for seventeenth-century Puritanism is, I am sure, endlessly rehearsed in courses on the historiography of this period, since the debate over supposed links between economic base and some variety of intellectual structure in this period occupied generations of historians. Without making any broader claim, I think it is fair to say that population pressure was bringing changes in the English economy, putting pressure on individuals, families, villages to use the land more efficiently, to reclaim marshes and turn common land into enclosed farms, to select which crops to grow with an eye to the market, not just the sustenance of the local group, and was sending individuals away from their homes to nearby larger towns, to London, and even across the seas to Ireland, to the West Indies, and to North America.

On the *Arbella*, leading the way to New England, John Winthrop wrote his lay sermon, "A Model of Christian Charity." His image of the settlement he was coming to lead was the opposite of the individual's quest for profit. "We must be knit together in this work as one man. We must entertain each other in brotherly affection. . . . We must delight in each other, make others' conditions our own, rejoice together, mourn together, labor and suffer together." The rules Winthrop established in New England, which limited prices workmen and farmers could charge, followed this principle.

This is another meaning of space. In Winthrop's image the Puritan settlement was the old English village idealized, stripped of its undertow of backbiting and gossip, denuded of its lingering pagan traditions, airbrushed of its cruelties. As a direct link to the Puritans' sense of chiliastic urgency, their social and economic organization was an effort to live as Christians would after the defeat of the Antichrist. In this sense religious perfectionism was social utopianism. It offered a balm to those buffeted by change by promising a haven of communal concern. We often read of Islamic fundamentalist groups who offer social services, but I wonder if this broader link is there as well—the sense that the tensions of modern life would be eased in a tightly run community, especially after the final defeat of the forces of change.

But this picture of Puritan resistance to social and economic change leaves out the issue that has animated scholars since Max

Weber: how their ideal of being in the world but not of it perfectly suited the Godly to a new economic environment.

While Puritan rhetoric opposed many of the social and economic alterations in English life and proposed a utopian alternative to them, Puritan life often involved an embrace of disciplined industry, individual responsibility, contractual rather than status-based relationships, all of which were particularly well suited to the new economic and social circumstances.

Similarly, when pressed by Roger Williams on what right the English had to own land in America at all, since it belonged to the Indians and was not the king's to give away, Winthrop gave a singularly aggressive and "modern" argument. The Indians, he claimed, had not made any use of the land, they had not improved it, so they did not deserve it. His communal village in which each would care for the other, also staked its claim to the New World on how rapidly it could conquer the wilderness. In his *Messiah* Handel quotes Isaiah on "making straight the highway." This is a religious image, but it soon also became Puritan practice. In the name of preparing for the ultimate change just ahead, they led the way in altering their circumstances in their own time.

This is what I mean about the Puritans discerning that they were living in a changed world, and even in a sense leading the way into that new social and economic environment, even as their rhetoric and their interpretation of their sacred narrative claimed that they were resisting innovations, wiping away error, and returning to a purified life.

I have already heard from a number of friends who are knowledgeable about modern Islam that a similar argument has been made about "fundamentalist" groups. Their focus on self-discipline, use of new banking techniques, embrace of technology are quite "modern." Even the focus on women wearing body coverings is a way to cope with, and allow, more women into public life. The parallel question, then, is what changes are the fundamentalists in particular attuned to? What adaptations are they initiating in the name of resistance?

The bigger question I would pose here is psychological. The aspect of seventeenth-century Puritanism that I have found most fascinating is their understanding of personal psychology. The crucial moment for a Puritan was when he or she felt God's grace working in the heart or soul. Eventually Puritan divines would map out the five stages of this inner journey quite carefully. Winthrop's autobiography distills the key moment to its essence. A disciplined, hardworking man made endless resolutions to do better, to live a more godly life. But no matter how hard he tried, he always failed. He saw that he must give up the world, and that, as a creature of the world, he could not. "There was never any holy meditation, prayer, or action that I had a hand in," he realized, that truly succeeded. All that was left was complete submission to God. "I neither hope nor desire to stand by mine own strength, wisdom, etc., but only by faith in Christ Jesus." Just when he lost hope of making any spiritual progress on his own, God "filled me with such power of faith, sense of his love, etc., as has made my heart melt with joy."

Giving up hope of doing anything by his personal will allowed him to feel God's caress, the touch of divine spirit. First he felt the wash of healing mercy, then he saw how he must live, then he became a full member of the community of other saints who had had similar experiences. From despair he was led to hope, community, and a clear direction in life.

The genius of this understanding is that it made all of human doubt, despair, self-loathing a necessary part of the process of salvation. This made it a perfect inner mechanism for people being buffeted by changes in their lives, by difficult economic conditions and shifting social circumstances. All of these outer forces were sure to inspire inner questioning. Instead of telling people filled with a lacerating sense of their own weakness and sinfulness to just come to church, listen to the nice bishop in his pretty robe, and obey the good king with his Catholic wife, the Puritans said, "What you are experiencing is exactly what a potentially saved person must go through. Face it squarely and you may yet feel the breath of God."

Critics of the Puritans, then and now, find this emphasis on inner doubt and self-condemnation evidence of their dour, judgmental, harsh outlook. They had those traits. But they also understood people's inner life and offered a passage past emotions people could not simply dismiss, confess, or salve through ritual. No wonder that the greatest artistic creation to come out of the Puritan period is Milton's *Paradise Lost*, which made vivid the psychology of the rebel, of Lucifer, who rejected God. This is the side of the self the Puritans mapped.

But how did this inner experience relate to outward acts? This was a crucial, perhaps even insoluble, matter for the Puritans especially when they were in power, and it leads me to the next question I would ask the Islamicists here. In England, Puritans rejected the Church of England for falling into Arminianism, the false belief that your actions in the world were any guide at all to the status of your soul. If a person had not been touched by inner spirit, the most exemplary life could be simply a perfect hypocrisy. But in America Puritans faced the opposite challenge. When Anne Hutchinson apparently claimed direct revelations from God, they accused her of falling into the heresy of antinomianism. An inner voice could well be diabolical, especially if it led to divisions in the community and disparaged its leaders.

The resolution the Puritans came to in New England, in which increments of good behavior in your public life were taken as a sign of the influence of spirit in your inner life, seems to me the only realistic answer they could have come to, and also a betrayal of the deepest wellsprings of their faith. Which is another way of saying that I personally find Puritanism more interesting as a form of psychology than as a basis for government. The endless ink spilled on the putative decline of Puritans into Yankees traces out the course of this very issue.

As I understand it, Islamic fundamentalism focuses more on outward acts, on conformity to a code of behavior, than it does on the state of your soul when you perform those acts. The question, then, is how it functions in the inner psychology of its adherents. Like seventeenth-century Puritanism it seems to offer eschatological hope, a sense of community with other believers, a vision of shared life that wipes away the stresses of modern life, and yet access to various contemporary technological and social mechanisms. But what does it offer for one's inner life? Is there something in the focus on liberation through submission that parallels the Puritans' psychological insight?

We often read that people in the Islamic world have experienced a series of humiliations from the outside, in the decline of Islamic empires, the rise of the West, the period of colonial control of the Middle East, defeats by Israel, America's wars and global influence.

In political terms, Islam is being asked to submit, to bow to the West. Yet Islam also seems to offer strength in submission to its followers, in submission to Allah. How do these two opposed but perhaps linked senses of submission interact? Submission and aggression now, just as the Puritans experienced humiliation and salvation then, are psychological pairs that are worth exploring.

The last topic I thought we might consider today comes out of the news. The Puritans were as preoccupied with the Holy Land as either ultra-Orthodox Israelis or those Muslims for whom Jerusalem is the central issue. The difference is that they assumed the sacred space had shifted and was now either England or New England. They read the very passages I discussed at Passover last week, but applied them to their own errand in the wilderness of the New World. The Land of Promise was literally the one discussed in the Bible, it just did not happen to be in the same place anymore. Thus one of the Puritans' justifications for not being too concerned about the rights of the people already living in New England is that they were the Canaanites.

Because the Puritans treated the story of exodus and redemption as literal truth, but placed it in a different locale, it made me think about the special circumstances we have now in the Middle East, where there are simultaneous issues of place and of metaphor. In other words, one set of conflicts is ultimately about water rights, contiguous or noncontiguous Palestinian territories, borderlines between states, the number of Israeli settlements that are permitted to remain. These are issues of place that could arise anywhere. But another is about sacred narratives, about prophecy and the end of time. The place is the staging area for ultimate things. The Puritans' good fortune is that they could relinquish, or transmute, their prophetic sense of America, until it came to reside on our dollar bills as The New Order of Man. Today, unfortunately, the place and the metaphor are the same.

The last question I would then pose is to what degree those two problems are inextricably entangled today and whether they can be delinked. Is there any way within the languages of extreme Judaism or fundamentalist Islam that could allow the sacred narrative of place to be deliteralized, so that the place becomes secular, even as the story of ultimate things remains vibrant?

Chapter 8

The Crucible: Witch-Hunt and Religion, Crossing Point of Many Histories

I wrote two versions of this essay, and a combined, edited version of them appears as the epilogue to my forthcoming book, Witch-Hunt: Mysteries of the Salem Witch Trails *(Atheneum, 2003). I am grateful to Ginee Seo at Atheneum for permitting me to use this draft here, and for challenging questions and observations as I was working on it. To round out the personal side of this book, my father worked with both Arthur Miller and Elia Kazan, designed the original sets for* The Crucible, *and strongly sided with Miller after the events I describe here. The heroic story of Miller's courage in refusing to name names to the House Un-American Activities Committee was frequently recounted at our kitchen table. I suppose hearing that so often as a child influences me to this day, encouraging me to believe it is more important for all of us to speak the truth as we see it than to be accepted by even our most respected, or powerful, peers.*

In classrooms across this land, Arthur Miller's play *The Crucible* is treated as a kind of direct view across the centuries into the hearts and minds of the Puritans and farmers of colonial New England. That is a mistake. And yet the play is a brilliant creation, well worth the attention it gets. The real question that should be preoccupying teachers and students is why *The Crucible* is such a compelling portrait of a witch-hunt if it does not draw its power from insight into the events of 1692? What is the truth that the play captures if it is not the specifics of the Salem trials? The answers to these questions make Miller's creation all the more relevant to young people now, in the wake of the September 11th attacks, than it would be if it were merely a cleverly written history lesson.

Having at his command in 1952 only a well-written but unreliable nineteenth-century local history and the popular but inaccurate *The Devil in Massachusetts* by Marion Starkey, as well as the original pretrial transcripts which themselves contain subtle errors close readers have since corrected, Miller was wrong about some of his facts; he consciously combined characters, and the main lines of his interpretations do not match the views of modern historians. To take a glaring example, even when he published his autobiography *Timebends* in 1987, Miller wrote that, "I had no doubt that Tituba, Reverend Parris's black Bardados slave, had been practicing witchcraft" (all Miller quotations in this essay are from *Timebinds*). Since the early seventies when an English professor carefully reread the original sources, scholars have known that Tituba was an Indian, not an African, and that if she used any ritual or folk magic at all, she learned the practices from her English neighbors and owners. Anyone who would like to see a listing of all of the historical errors in Miller's play can go to sites such as ogram.org/17thc/miller.shtml where they are neatly spelled out, with links to other sites that go into even more detail.

Despite these historical "flaws," the "gotcha" satisfaction of pointing out places where the play does not match the historical record is a cheap and easy victory. It is a triumph of easy erudition that makes the critic the superior mind for seeing mistakes, without granting to Miller his true achievement: his ability to make us believe he has it right.

The Crucible should be used in classrooms as a wonderful example of historical fiction, not because it is fiction that teaches us history, but because its very historical limitations show us the power of fiction to create a scene that feels real, vivid, true. Accuracy to events does not make historical fiction ring true. The more you know about the historical record, the more you appreciate Miller's ability to create characters who *ought* to have existed, even if they didn't, stories that you *know* to be true, even if they weren't. His confident and insightful sense of psychology, his thoughtful, well-researched scene-setting, and his deft characterization are all testimony to his greatness as a writer, not his deep knowledge or profound understanding of the past.

A writer has the ability to render something that feels three-dimensional, that feels real. For some reason many people, from teachers, parents, and book reviewers to talk show hosts associate this artistic ability, this mastery of craft and technique, with a moral quality—a manner of truth-telling that is grounded in the world outside of art. In other words, if you are good, sincere, honest, and true that will shine through in your book. And if your historical novel is absolutely faithful to fact, readers will experience it as a vivid portrait of the past. Like Hollywood costume designers who used to make sure stars in movie biographies wore historically accurate underwear, getting the hats, buttons, and turns of phrase right is seen as a sign that you really care about the past, which will make your novel "good."

The Crucible puts the lie to this view. It reminds us that at least half of historical fiction, the "fiction" part, is pure invention. Miller's play is good because he makes the world he has invented come alive, not because it captures life as it actually was lived.

The Crucible is, though, not simply a triumph of artistry. As Miller so vividly explains in *Timebends*, he saw an obvious link between the activities of the House Un-American Activities Committee, which, in the early 1950s, was relentlessly pursuing tales of a vast Communist conspiracy in America, and the trials as portrayed in Starkey's book. "The main point," he realized, "of the hearings, precisely as in seventeenth-century Salem, was that the accused make public confession, damns his confederates as well as his Devil master, and guarantee his sterling new allegiance by breaking disgusting old vows—whereupon he was let loose to rejoin the society of extremely decent people." Miller saw the trials as a kind of ritual cleansing, in which guilt could be released through confession and naming other sinners. That insight into the structure of the Salem hearings is true, or at least is true of a phase of the trials, once accused witches began to confess. Probing into his own time, Miller understood the psychodynamics of the past, even if he did not get the details entirely right.

Miller had a subject that could speak to a current crisis while illuminating a fascinating historical moment, but what should the play be? He had an image in mind, via the character of John Proctor, a good man who had once had an affair with a seventeen-year-old maid, and now had to face her leading a pack of accusers that was taking aim at his own wife. At that time Miller had entered psychoanalysis because he was haunted by the mutual attraction he and Marilyn Monroe had felt when they met briefly in Hollywood. Though he had not yet begun a relationship with Monroe, he felt that he was betraying his own marriage, both by continuing to live a lie and through his desire for Monroe. Procter might well have been a fictional depiction of Miller's dilemma. The development of the play also emerged out of his own life.

As he was about to leave to go to Salem to read the pretrial transcripts, Miller received a call from the brilliant film director Elia Kazan. Miller knew, even as he drove to Kazan's Connecticut home, what he was about to hear. To save his career in Hollywood, Kazan had joined the modern witch-hunt. He had spoken to HUAC, and given them the names of people he claimed had once been Communists. Miller was not shocked, but he was angry. "It was not his (Kazan's) duty to be stronger than he was, the government had no right to require anyone to be stronger than it had been given him to be, the government was not in that line of work in America. I was experiencing a bitterness with the country that I had never even imagined before, a hatred of its stupidity and its throwing away of its freedom. Who or what was safer now because this man in his human weakness had been forced to humiliate himself? What truth had been enhanced by all this anguish?"

Miller was later called to Washington, too, and pressured to give them more names, more people to pressure into confessions. He refused. That made his conversation with Kazan all the more intense. The conversation of a man who bowed to the committee, and another who was determined to resist them was a drama fully as powerful as any either would place on the stage. And it gave Miller the vision of what his play would be about: "the shifts of interests that turned loving husbands and wives into stony enemies, loving parents into indifferent supervisors or even exploiters of their children. As I already knew from my reading, that was the real story of ancient Salem Village, what they called the breaking of charity with one another."

Miller was again right. The Break with Charity is what drove the trials forward, as it did the HUAC hearings, and it is what to-day we must be on guard against as we change laws to accom-modate a state of war against terror. *The Crucible* should be taught as fine writing, but also as an insight into how a witch-hunt works. When each of our comfort, safety, fear of being ac-cused, and even justified anger at an enemy allows us to sup-press doubt, and silence the voice of humanity that lets us identify with prisoners, suspects, accused evil-doers, then we are in real danger of doing evil ourselves. Miller's triumph was in creating a kind of psychological realism that did not depend at all on its historical setting. And that is how I think we should treat it today.

Miller has identified one last source for *The Crucible*, and that adds a final twist to this tangle of personal and national history, personal insight and literary accomplishment. At the Historical Society in Danvers he saw etchings of court scenes, perhaps from the trials. In the faces of the bearded judges recoiling from the ag-onized accusers he suddenly saw his own religious Jewish for-bears. Salem was not just about America's Puritan, Protestant past, it was about "the moral intensity of the Jews and the clan's defensiveness against pollution from outside the ranks. I under-stood Salem in that flash, it was suddenly my own inheritance."

The Crucible is great because Miller penetrated the psychology of a political witch-hunt, and because it speaks about a moment in the life of a people aching to reach toward God and to protect themselves from evil. That, too, is in the headlines today. And a version of that same insight drew me to the Salem story. In the struggles of the Puritans to remain true to their faith in a time of increasing doubt, I saw my own rabbi grandfather, none of whose ten children were devout. That association made me sympathetic to the strains the Puritans experienced, while for Miller it explained their ferocious intensity.

If fiction can give us insights that transcend time—offering us a picture of the witch-hunt mentality that was true of the 1950s America in which it was written, and the seventeenth-century Salem it describes, and holding out a caution to us in 2002—history can do something else. On the one hand it reminds us of particularity and difference, and that is where Miller got it wrong. The more we know about witchcraft beliefs in the seventeenth century the less they resemble the sexually driven fears and passions of his play. On the other hand, though, as we study the objects and records left behind from the past, we make sense of them by examining our own ideas, memories, and images. We see ourselves through the past, and the past through ourselves. In the process both are modified. Being the product of the great struggle over modernization in Judaism made the struggles over modernization in the seventeenth century much more interesting to me, as it did for Miller.

History is a mirror, fiction a portrait. If Miller's painting has a few characters wrong, it still shows a great deal of truth, and his reflections cast wide, into unexpected places. That is a great accomplishment and should give classrooms much to talk about for generations to come.

Chapter 9

Biography and Its Perils

This essay is, in a sense, the reverse of the previous one. There I stressed the fictional value in historical fiction, even when it is not historically accurate. Here I describe the reading satisfactions that biographies offer precisely because they are so hard to write.

I see biography in two different but linked ways—depending on whether I am viewing it with my writer/reader sensibility or my editor/publisher judgment. As an author, biography presents a magnificent opportunity that I cannot imagine finding in any other type of creative writing. For to capture a life on paper, especially for younger readers, involves all of the narrative promise of historical fiction, with all of the knowledge of a time generally found in adult monographs. When biography lives up to that challenge, it is one of my favorite reading experiences. The hard part is that while biography has this high calling, it has a bad rap. It is too often celebrated for how it can be *used*, not for what it *does*. Library shelves are crammed with "serviceable" works that "meet a need" and are "good for reports." And bookstores can be even worse, for there are very few shelves available in which to fit all of those competing books.

If I have one goal in this essay it is to awaken the sense of what biography can be. There is a dilemma every biographer faces, and how he or she resolves that difficult problem is the heart of the book. Yet this magnificent challenge is so little recognized that the entire genre is too often viewed as dull—an inferior second choice a writer takes on because fiction is too hard. If anything, those terms should be reversed. Fiction, especially historical fiction, can be the recourse of the author afraid to write a biography.

Here's the crux of the biographer's challenge: you are writing about a person because you find him or her interesting in some way, and because his or her time is fascinating. You are using the life to explain the time. But, from the very first sentence, you need to evoke the time in order to make sense of the life. There is no clear, consistent, formulaic way to do both of these things at the same time. In fact, there is no way ever to get it totally right. But for that very reason, every biography should have a freshness, a creativity, an interesting tension that makes it different from every other one.

Life and time are inextricably linked. That is why you are writing about a figure from the past, rather than a journalistic piece about a contemporary. Without context, the subject's actions may make no sense, his or her emotions and reactions may seem simply odd, especially to young readers. In turn, the environment in which this life was lived had rules, beliefs, structures of family, schooling, faith that will often be completely new to your audience. How do you set the scene and tell the story—which explains the scene—at the same time?

Authors writing picture book biographies have images on every page that place a reader in the setting, like a diorama at a museum. But in exchange for this gift they have such low word counts that the author almost has to write a historical poem rather than a true biography. In some middle-grade biographies, the spreads are filled with endless sidebars, background printed computer-generated images, and other design derring-do put there to make a book appear to be a magazine or a catalog. This evades the biographer's task, since the artifacts of the time essentially supplant the life. The life is merely an excuse to feature the material culture that has survived from the period.

In a true biography, especially for readers from grades six or seven up, each word stands alone—with perhaps an archival image every few pages to give a flavor of the time and place. These words are something like the world as experienced by the two-dimensional people in Flatland. They have to signify a three-dimensional world—that past environment in which the person lived and acted, how it looked, smelled, sounded, felt, what thoughts people thought, what feelings they felt, what ideas they debated, discussed, fought over, and changed. They must carry all of that information while simultaneously describing the progress of a life completely embedded in that time.

It is this dual obligation to life and time that, I believe, sends people eagerly to historical fiction. There, they hope the dressing, the costume, of the past will cloak a life whose basic nature we identify with and understand. That way we can absorb interesting and telling details, while being carried along by physical, emotional, spiritual, psychic challenges that we can easily grasp. The problem is that using fiction in this way to avoid the biographer's dilemma hurls you into the historical fiction writer's trap. The truer you are to the time, the less likely that the character you create will resemble the reader. The more weight you place on making the characters appealing, familiar, emotionally contemporary, the less likely they are to be true to their own time. So while turning to fiction makes it easier to please the reader, it then sets up the kinds of problems that critics and teachers endlessly wrangle about: How accurate is this book? How useful is it in a school setting?

Because the biographer does not have the novelist's freedom, he or she is actually in a better position. What you cannot evade, you must meet head on. And here is where a biographer has great freedom, a great opportunity to be creative, and a magnificent opportunity to give a rare gift to young readers. The biographer can begin at any point in the life: beginning, middle, high point, low point, even at the end. He or she can evoke the entire life and time through a single event, or trace the slow unfolding of a sensibility. The author can use an exciting moment that really happened to expand or to reveal the fundamental issues of a time. Or he or she can begin with a broad overview—like a voice-over in an old historical movie—then swoop down on the character in midaction.

The adult biographer does not have as interesting a challenge, for he or she can assume the reader knows enough about the period to make sense of the character. We in children's books cannot be so cavalier, which is why some adults secretly like to read nonfiction written for younger readers.

So how can it be that a genre whose very nature pushes authors to be innovative is hard to sell? All too often authors and publishers settle. In the past they were willing to sacrifice historical accuracy and complexity for some supposed moral lesson. Biography was really a form of hagiography, a saint's life that was meant to inspire young readers to live better. Today, utility more than morality can call the tune. A biography is treated as a tool for the classroom, not as a branch of literature.

Yet we cannot take all of the blame ourselves. There is a bias towards fiction throughout the children's book world that assumes that the only place young readers will find well-crafted narratives is in novels. If writers and editors settle, too many teachers, librarians, and booksellers are willing to let them.

Children are growing up swimming in a flood of information: facts, images, sounds, sights, and sites. The great literature of biography offers them a model of how to piece together all of these disparate details into a story that explains a person and his or her time. I cannot think of a more interesting, more important, more relevant task for an author.

Section 4

TEEN TROUBLES: THE CHALLENGES OF PUBLISHING FOR ADOLESCENT READERS

Chapter 10

The Pursuit of Happiness: Does American History Matter?

This essay follows from the previous one. It explores in one very specific way how I think we have failed to write good history for our readers. As I showed in the Columbia talk on the Puritans and modern Islamic fundamentalism, I think we always need to see our history in a global perspective. But we also need to define what it is that matters in our history.

I am grateful to have been invited here to speak with you about nonfiction and the ways in which it can be creative while remaining true to its calling, which is to be true. A study released earlier this month, however, completely changed what I had planned to say. The National Assessment of Educational Progress report showed that young Americans know almost nothing about our own history. Two-thirds of fourth graders know the basics of American history that are appropriate to their age. Not horrible, but still it is of serious concern that one-third of fourth graders do not have this baseline knowledge, and it gets worse from there. The rate of ignorance climbs with age. The number of students not able to marshal the minimum knowledge level rises to 36 percent by eighth grade, and 57 percent in the last year of high school. Remember, this is an index of how many students do not know enough to *pass* the test. Looking at the same question

in reverse—how many young people have "solid academic performance"—the numbers go from alarming to devastating. Eighteen percent of fourth graders, 17 percent of eighth graders, and
a mere 10 percent of seniors—those who are closest to becoming
voters—are what we might call B students of the history, traditions, ideas, and values that created this nation.

These numbers are an indictment of our schools, of our society
and its values, of our textbooks, but also of us. I want to use this
chance to talk with you about what we have and have not done
to cause this complete failure of our ability to pass on the meaning of our own past to our children, and what we can do to remedy it. American history matters a great deal to me, but the failure the report exposes goes beyond this subject, and so what I
hope we discuss and learn today matters whether or not you
write nonfiction, or write for children, or write at all.

The NAEP survey did not address the reasons for the failure,
but it did include one telling statistic. Nearly 54 percent of high
school history teachers had no training in the field, a degree of
pedagogical ignorance exceeded only in physics, where the
number was over 56 percent. The image of the rigid, thick, dull
gym teacher who doubles up in history that I've seen satirized
in YA novels turns out to be true. Why is that so? How come
history has been seen as so easy, or unimportant, that anyone
with a textbook and a lesson plan can get by? And why is it that
so few truly knowledgeable people are motivated to teach?

I have one rather odd but probably apt culprit to add to the
usual list of suspects: the success of feminism. As long as bright,
motivated women had limited educational and career opportunities, we had an endlessly self-renewing supply of talented
women in their twenties who would go to state "normal"
schools, learn how to teach, spend a few years at it, and then get
married and have a family. Many of those women, I am sure,
would have become doctors, lawyers, politicians, professors,
CEOs if those paths were available. But as they were not, or were
so hard to reach that only the most fortunate or motivated
women could go after them—perhaps at the sacrifice of family
life—students got the benefit of unusually talented teachers.
Now we have the opposite situation. Almost every career path is

open to women, so why would a woman choose to take the lower paying, less prestigious, more thankless task of being a teacher? The opening up of opportunity for women reduced the potential teacher pool down to those who are completely committed to education, or those less motivated women, the very kinds of people unlikely to seek extra training in a subject area. There are some exceptions to this, and our children, especially in urban areas, may benefit from this for a generation or so: immigrant women who come from countries which value education, but who do not feel as confident about pursuing professional or managerial careers, may become teachers in higher numbers. Their relationship to American history is likely to be less cynical, and more appreciative, than many native-born Americans. Though the view of American history may not be the same, there probably is some parallel in the case of nonwhite women whose path to advancement may be more obstructed.

So if underfunding and large-scale gender shifts undermine the schools, what about society in general? Why don't we as a culture, as a nation, value our past? Here I think my generation, our generation, is at fault. In the sixties when I was coming of age, it was very exciting to challenge the American history we grew up with. We were, in a sense, living a teenage version of a long *Our Gang* episode. As some of you may recall, in that show, Spanky, Alfalfa, Buckwheat, and the rest made fun of the pretentious, long-winded, irrelevance of Arbor Day ceremonies and other nineteenth-century school relics. Similarly, as radical students, we could punch holes in the sanitized Hollywood Pageant of America story we heard and saw all the time, gleefully revealing how women, or slaves, or workers, or Jews, or Hispanics were left out or stereotyped. Our great cause was bottom-up history, history of the common people, history of every distinct group. And we had a second cause, which you might call the value of fun. As devotees of rock 'n' roll, we argued that popular culture was as real, as true, as important as high culture. We were making mischief with W. C. Fields and Spanky, not nodding in agreement with the sententious teacher.

From the seventies on, via *Roots*, and the subsequent boom in memoir, family history, media studies on one side, and the culture wars splitting apart every discipline into hyphenated sub-disciplines on the other, our team won. We won so completely that any unified sense of American history was lost. We have a history channel, we have movies on Pearl Harbor, and *A League of Their Own*, we have a steady diet of Ken and Rick Burns documentaries, but we have no sense that any of this matters to all of us. Any patriotic sense of the meaning and purpose of our history feels like the bunting trotted out for conventions, the World Series, or some anniversary—for a second we can get a twinge of the old emotions, but it quickly passes. Everything feels canned, planned, two-dimensional. We just don't really care.

We sort of know and believe that this country has something to do with freedom and liberty, but we are so aware of how that is not so, and so cynical about the ways those phrases are bandied about by interest groups, that the terms have no meaning. There are those who trumpet about history, but the Left does so to undermine and challenge the present in ways that often feel dated, while the Right counters with flag waving designed to deflect these attacks and glorify the present, without examining it.

I was prompted to think about the feeling about our past that we have lost by seeing a recent movie from India called *Legaan*, or *The Tax*. It is a wide-screen, all-singing, all-dancing, fictionalized version of a true event in their colonial history, when a group of Indians beat the Brits at cricket, and so staved off a crippling tax. It is the kind of fun and yet heartwarming and inspiring movie we made about our own past in the fifties. It is the kind of movie we could not make today because we know too much about that past.

After we grant the weakness of the schools and the general cultural shift in which we have lost any sense of what it is about our collective past, all of our American history, that matters, the finger turns to us. We are writers and editors and publishers who are not beholden to the school system. I at least have no expectation that my books will be adopted and used in class. I write them as I please, for the bookstore and library market. Why is it that we have failed to provide books that inspire young people to care about our history? What have we done wrong?

I think we have fallen into a number of traps, all of which are related to our own lack of faith in the importance, interest, relevance of history. One trap is to give kids neatly packaged history, as is done in series books, or even stand-alone volumes by famous historians. There is no imagination in these books; the predictable facts, dates, photos, and maps tell the same old stories in essentially the same old ways. These books are not bad, but they are limited. They are a kind of McDonald's history: easy to use, predictable, but not sustaining.

Another trap is the sense that we must tell a single history about one point of view or experience—write about a white woman or a black man, write about a Latino movement or Rosie the Riveter. We are endlessly recycling those sixties victories, bringing to light all of the ignored and forgotten. This was at one point a healthy corrective. It was bad that there were so few books about important, heroic, successful, dynamic people in our past who were not WASPs. In general I think the whole focus on books by and about members of a specific group has done some good in that it encouraged the development of some authors and artists and fostered the growth of a needed literature. But this approach also splinters history. It forgets that there is also a history of connection, of commonality, of interaction.

At Cricket Books we are just now working on a book on the evidence, the archaeology and written record, of the Underground Railroad. That is a history of abolitionists *and* slaves, not one or the other. It is a joint history. People of all races made choices, to escape or to stay, to betray or to keep silent, to assist or ignore. That is a history about all of us that matters to all of us; it is not a part of black history or white history. When I wrote about Sir Walter Ralegh I was fascinated at how he saw America as a virgin land, which meant he urgently wanted to possess, to rape it, and to protect, to honor it. He had both powerful drives. I suspect that this mix of emotions was what many Europeans felt in those early days.

As the Ralegh case shows, I am explicitly *not* saying that we need a pretty history, a proud history, a history that leaves out or plays down the stories of the destructive wars with Indian peoples, of slavery, of the internment camps, of anti-Semitism, nativism, labor conflict, etc. We were absolutely justified, back in the sixties, in exposing these gaps in the stories we were told in school. But the problem is that we have not found out how to say anything more than that. For me to have described Ralegh's lust to conquer the new land and not his yearning to protect it would be as wrong as to write of him as a bearer of civilization without mentioning his savagery.

I think the next challenge for us as writers is to look at our history in new ways, beyond, as it were, black and white. This relates to the theme I had originally intended to discuss, creative nonfiction. Part of the pressure authors feel to fictionalize history, or dramatize moments, or remove any hint of research from their books, is the fear that otherwise the book will not be interesting. The implication behind this is that history in itself is boring. Or that kids feel that way so strongly that we need to use tricks, devices, glitter and glitz, to get them to pay attention. Popular culture is, well, so popular, that we despair of making the past matter as it actually took place, so we try to make it as un-past-like as we can: dressing modern characters up in old-fashioned clothes.

The problem of presentation, and of competing with popular culture comes up most starkly, I think, in the issue of art and design. Here it is not entirely our fault. In an age where young people have access to a broad spectrum of primarily visual stimuli—TV, Internet, DVD, digital games, magazines, graphic novels—it is hard to be confident about a book filled with text. And yet, while so many images are available for kids to look at, clip, download for free, we have to pay hefty permission fees to reproduce them in books. This squeezes nonfiction into topics popular enough to pay high fees, or to those with cheap art, or to shorter books. I think our copyright system is broken in this regard, punishing authors of serious books with small print runs, and rewarding online providers of far less well-crafted materials. I would like to see some kind of mixed educational/trade exemption, where a nonfiction book for younger readers that is not a textbook, but clearly is in some form instructional, could pay, say, a heavily discounted fee, or a small royalty to some educational fund. This would not diminish the copyright claims of the rights holders, but would do what copyright is meant to do, which is to encourage creativity.

Our concern to offer a single exemplar to each kind of young person, and our fear of boring young readers comes together in an unhealthy package. We seek to engage readers rather than to inspire them, and if we offer stories of heroism, ideals, and accomplishment they are about one or another individual, not about broader themes characterizing our history as a whole.

We have meekly settled into writing books that fit into series formats, or give bits and bites of history, or splinter history, for our own reasons. I think this shows our own lack of faith. We are not sure what matters about our history so we cannot communicate that to young people. When I was in high school we used a textbook that was precisely the sort of book we then ripped to shreds. It was called *History of a Free People*. Ok, which free people? I'm sure all of you can name which Americans that did not describe. If we were today to write a book for young people, if all of us in this room sat down together to create a book on the history of freedom, of the struggle for freedom, of the idea of freedom, in American history, I think we'd have a great deal of trouble deciding how to do it. We'd either think we were sanitizing, or we'd lose our way in the exceptions. It would be easier just to write a novel about a young boy at Valley Forge, a girl on the home front during the Civil War.

But if we don't have a sense of why our history matters, of what it adds up to, of why our nation exists, what it stands for, how it got that way, then why should kids care? The staggering numbers in the survey are, in the end, a good reflection of our own uncertainties. I say that with respect, because challenging the old verities was good. It is just that we have not moved on beyond the challenge. We have not, as my doctoral adviser once pointed out, figured out what the whole of our history is, now that we have broken it down into parts.

The creativity I think we need in nonfiction, at least nonfiction about American history, is in our own thinking about our own history. We as educated adults who are good communicators must decide for ourselves what America is so that we feel it important to explain how it got that way. And I believe we can.

We are doing a book for teenagers called *911: The Book of Hope*. It is a collection of essays, poems, autobiographical pieces, short stories all related to the attacks. As I described in chapter four, I was inspired to create it by the intensely moving experience of attending a spontaneous memorial service on the Friday of the attack. That was an exceptional moment, which Russell Freedman writes about in our book. And that gathering reminded all of us that we do have some sense of what America means. It means the struggle for rights, but the defense of rights, it means room for faith, but tolerance of all beliefs, it means that we value brotherhood even if we must be conscious of how often we violate that imperative. These are the simple, self-evident truths we learned as kids, and they are what we all spontaneously turned to, and held onto, in the face of attack. I am sure that you here in Washington had similar soul-searching, similar reminders of your core values and beliefs. I urge you then to ask how you can communicate those convictions that we take so for granted that we need not even articulate them to younger people. How can you do so without being false to history, without becoming cliché-ridden, bombastic, preachy, without losing your integrity as writers?

The September 11th attacks exposed a kind of duality in our sense of this country. While we all acknowledge its failings, we have a kind of hidden, baseline sense of its value that we are somehow unable to articulate and express. We enjoy the present but are almost embarrassed, shy, awkward, about linking that to anything significant about our past. We are glad to be free to pursue our own visions of happiness; we see America as a good place in which to do so, and a bad place when it prevents us, or others, from having that opportunity. But we do not see those opportunities as being the result of a history in which that pursuit was a contested right.

When we began singing Civil Rights songs it was a reminder that that struggle for freedom was an American effort, not a black, or Jewish, or young people's cause. It was an effort by a broad spectrum of Americans to take our history seriously. When Martin Luther King began his speech at the Lincoln Memorial, his theme was to be about the unfulfilled promise of America. Midway through, he spontaneously shifted to speaking about his dream of America. It is that dream that we often return to, but it is equally important that we remind children about the promise, the link between the past, the founding ideals, of this nation, and the present.

America is a nation founded on ideas, it is not merely the location of a group of people who settled there over time, united by a mythic past, or a faith, or an ethnicity. The story of the contest over those ideas, the expansion of their application, the struggle to define their meaning, is our history. This is a grand subject for all of us.

We need better teachers, we need better-funded schools, we need innovative ways to present our ideas to kids immersed in visual stimulation. But as reflective, critical, thinking adults we also need to define what America, the contentious drama of America's past, means to us. Otherwise our books will be as empty, silent, dull as the copybooks of those nine-tenths of our high school seniors, who had less than a B-level knowledge of our past. That is the fine challenge we face as writers and as citizens, one that tests us, but which I think we will all be proud to tackle.

Chapter 11

Teenagers Don't Want to Read about Teen Angst, So Why Are So Many Angst-Filled Books Published?

At the 2002 annual meeting of the American Library Association in Atlanta, a large group of local teenagers were slated to come meet with the Best Books for Young Adults committee to give their views on the nominated titles. At the last minute they all canceled, summer and Sunday having taken their toll. But the intrepid librarians managed to round up a good selection of other teenagers, some from as far away as Michigan and North Carolina, who were attending the conference. Since these young people had not been prepped for the meeting, they had read only a few of the books under consideration, and we had time to fill. I decided to ask them about a favorite topic of mine, biography. I didn't like the answers I got, which made them all the more valuable.

The teenagers, mainly boys, said that they tended not to like biographies because they were too similar to the assigned reading they were given in school. Library reading, in other words, is leisure reading. For that reason they were drawn to fantasy, to science fiction, to graphic novels—books that were clearly different from the textbooks through which they must dutifully grind. This response is very similar to what Putnam editor Sharyn November says she has learned from her many meetings with teenagers, meetings that inspired her to create a fantasy line of her own, Firebird.

Recently Sharyn and I were sitting together at a meeting and she reiterated her point, adding with her own particular flair that, "I don't want to read about teen angst; that was my life."

So here's the dilemma: according to the teen readers in Atlanta, as well as those with whom Sharyn meets in the New York area, leisure reading should be fun, should be escape, should be as un-school and un-"my-life-is-hell," as possible. And yet, when you look at the manuscripts that flock to publishers in droves like birds migrating south, and that in smaller numbers issue forth from those same publishers as hardcovers and paperbacks, you see plenty of biographies—I write and publish them myself—and great numbers of books about adolescent misery. Why is that? Are we all wrong?

This question, the seeming mismatch between what teenagers want to read and what we publish, contains within it yet another question. And this second question is one that haunts many editors who publish YA books: do we have any responsibility to our readers, or is our obligation solely to our authors? Even as we struggle with that question, it arises in a different form in the author's mind. Is his or her goal to achieve on the page whatever artistic, creative, informing vision came in the middle of the night, or is the goal to select among such visions one that will reach, or be useful to, young readers, and then to craft it to achieve that goal?

In one sense we have authors writing and publishers publishing (sounds like the Twelve Days of Christmas) long biographies and soulful YA novels, and teenagers wanting fun and escape. It is easy to see the adults here as being in the wrong. In another sense we have authors searching their souls, struggling to be true to their creative visions, and publishers heroically ignoring the threat of failure and bringing forth these unique creations. Heedless teenagers, then, are challenged to put down their distractions and read difficult, important books. It is just as easy, here, to see the adults as being in the right.

Teenagers do, I am sure, want escape, entertainment, humor, distraction. Adults want these things, why shouldn't young adults? There *is* an odd joylessness in many YA books, and a strange, crashing absence of humor. The reasons for this may rest in the necessary generation gap involved in writing for teenagers: authors are mining their own adolescence, teenagers are living there. The two are related, but not the same.

Many authors write for teenagers or about adolescence because they experienced that time of life with particular intensity, and they want to pass on a crafted version of those vivid experiences to others—perhaps to help them, perhaps to help themselves, perhaps simply because these visions, memories, reflections seem so rich and intense any artist would be compelled to explore them. These motivations at least partially explain why we see so many angst-filled YA books. But these are inspirations for *creation;* they do not say anything about *transmission.* Just because one earnest adult writes it and another publishes it does not mean any teenager will want to read it, or that it would be "good" for him if he did.

An April 2001 article in the *Atlantic* by the author and essayist David Brooks provides one key to the puzzling dissonance between the standard YA book and the actual teenage readership. In analyzing current undergraduates at Princeton, Brooks quoted some amazing comparative statistics about teenagers. In 1974, 40 percent of teenagers surveyed wished they were not living with their parents, and a majority of them said they could not "comfortably approach their parents with personal matters of concern." Quite reasonably when those teenagers grew up, a good many of them felt a need to write down what they had never been able to express at home. By contrast, in 1997, an amazing 96 percent of teenagers said they got along with their parents, and 82 percent spoke of their home life as "wonderful" or "good."

The Princeton professors Brooks interviewed also kept shaking their heads about how unquestioning their students were, how ready to accept authority. Aaron Friedberg, a professor of international relations, reported that "it's very rare to get a student to challenge anything or to take a position that's counter to what the professor says." Graying authors like me, who write biographies for teenagers in part to inspire them to question everything, may be as out of touch as the author of yet another angst-filled YA novel.

In one way we might say that the YA books created in the eighties and after did their job: kids no longer have to hide much, adults are more ready to listen, both have books to bridge what-ever gaps remain. In another way, though, we see a statistical por-trait of the gap Sharyn has experienced anecdotally. If the early-to-mid-sixties teenagers faced a literature crafted out of the repressed fifties, twenty-first-century teenagers find shelves filled with the problems and attitudes of the last millennium. Maybe those frustrated seventies teenagers were reading utopian books about sixties' lives of questing and possibility, while seeing the grimmer consequences of much of that rebellion all around them.

This gap will never entirely go away, since books written by teenagers about their own time are generally weak in other ways—the authors simply do not yet have command of the medium of writing. Thus it will always take about a decade for an author to be ready to capture on paper what coming-of-age used to be like. Even Brooks's portrait of happy, driven, teenagers eagerly looking forward to taking their places in a booming economy seems hopelessly dated in these days of lengthening economic doldrums, appalling accounting scandals, terrorism, and war. An author who rushed to write a happy YA novel to please the teenagers of September 10, 2001, might well seem even more inappropriate to teenagers a year later than one of those authors who came of age in the eighties and was still coping with his wounds.

The very best writing for any age has a timeless quality that speaks to essential experiences that are not time-bound. Dedi-cated authors need the freedom to go where their talent de-mands, even if that is not territory certain to please most teenaged readers. We grant writers for adults this latitude, why not those who write for teenagers?

Stephen Roxburgh, the excellent editor and publisher at Front Street, has brought the world many award-winning novels by authors such as Carolyn Coman, Brock Cole, An Na, and Marilyn Nelson, precisely by sticking to his own inner aesthetic sense and not bending to any estimation of shifting teenage tastes.

One way, then, to bridge the generation gap is to write a book that is so true, so powerful, it captures the essence of ado-lescence, rather than the vagaries of growing up in one time or another.

But authors who aim at writing such books face one very daunting hurdle: it is very difficult to tell the world what they have done. I recently read Leonard Marcus's biography, *Margaret Wise Brown: Awakened by the Moon* and was struck by the difference between the world in which she published and the current scene. She and the illustrators she worked with assumed that in order to create good art for children they had both to be in constant contact with children *and* to pay close attention to the most advanced art of their time. Surrealism and constructivism, as well as hours working with kids at the Bank Street experimental school, influenced the illustrations of her books.

We have split those worlds apart. Some editors visit teenagers; others insist that publishing is part of contemporary high art. Though it is interesting that Sharyn often reprints in paperback the books Stephen first brings out in hardcover, so perhaps our publishing environment first splits and then reunites the two approaches to books for teenagers.

When they were published, Wise Brown's books were reviewed by critics in major publications, ranging from the *Horn Book* and other publications aimed at the institutional world to the *New Yorker* and the *New York Times*. Many of these critics looked at the art within the broader artistic context of the times. It was this sense that books for young readers were embedded within the larger literary scene that made it quite natural for Gertrude Stein to write books for children. Leading critics, artists, editors agreed that dreams, the surreal, the unconscious, the abstract were similar to the worlds of childhood, so it made sense for critics to take children's books seriously, and for creators to draw on the most advanced forms of art.

It is also, of course, true that in just this same period the stern institutional voice of Anne Carroll Moore ruled against many of Margaret Wise Brown's books. It is not that once upon a time there was a golden age in which books for young readers were always taken seriously. There have always been deep divisions among adults about what constitutes a good book for younger readers. Still, a book for younger readers had a better chance of being evaluated as literature and art and, in at least some places, read by the general public in the forties than it does now.

Today, we have absorbed books for young readers into a weird crossing point of the institutional and retail worlds. Books for young readers are to be useful, or broadly appealing. Books for teenagers achieve this utility by helping young people "cope," or by dealing with topics and themes covered in school.

Somehow we have managed to miss on both grounds: when kids want entertainment, we give them angst. When authors want to write about coming-of-age as part of the literature of our time, we judge their books on their utility and message. We have landed YA publishing in a blurry place where we applaud authors for reliving our adolescence in print, are generally out of touch with modern teenagers, and yet use "teen appeal" as a standard part of our judgment.

The key lesson of Marcus's biography and Brooks's essay is that both adolescence and the literature created for teenaged readers are historical constructs. Young people have different needs at different times; similarly, over time, the overlapping worlds of writing, publishing, reviewing, selling, and reading books adopt and evolve new definitions and standards for the literature of adolescence. The problem is that while all of this change is taking place we tend to act as if YA were a timeless category in which new generations continually read versions of more or less the same stories.

One reason for this assumption may be because, with a certain justice, we have taken that same approach to books for even younger readers. Generations of parents have believed, and been proven right, that each new youngster will like *Goodnight Moon*, or Mike Mulligan, or Dr. Seuss. We sort of know that teenagers are different, more in the here and now, more subject to trends. But we really haven't figured out how to apply that sense to how we create, review, and publish books for teenagers. And, I suspect, there is a deeper and more troubling source: our general willingness to freeze publishing categories in time, a lethal combination of inertia and arrogance that particularly afflicts us in publishing books for younger readers because the rest of the world ignores us.

I now live in a highly integrated middle-class suburb. Almost nowhere in books for young readers do I see my African

American neighbors, with their Lexus's in the driveway, their kids wearing helmets and skateboarding, dads getting off the commuter train after finishing their workdays in executive and managerial positions. And, as Ilan Stavans pointed out in *Wáchale,* his collection of Latino and Hispanic writings that we at Carus published in 2001, the literature of being Latino in America is overwhelmingly urban poor or rural/migrant.

In my essay on boys and reading (chapter thirteen), I note the gap between boys' love of cars and kids' books filled with barn animals. Link that up with the absence of middle-class life in books on African Americans or Latinos, and the overly alienated YA novels, and you have a portrait of an industry that slots books either towards the bucolic primitive or the urban tragic. The suburban is confined to middle grade and early YA books for girls about friendship, soccer, romance, and dating. The problem with dated YA topics is just one symptom of a broader malady.

We have not fully accepted the challenge that our profession necessarily poses for us: we are aiming to publish timeless literature for a readership defined by being in time. We want to say enduring things to readers who are, by definition, just now growing and changing. Not recognizing the profoundly complex nature of this challenge, one that is particularly difficult when we write and publish for teenagers, we settle for approximations. Childhood equals cows; teenage equals angst.

I think Sharyn is right that we editors need to get out more, and talk to, listen to, engage with more teenagers. My personal goal in this upcoming year is to do just that. I also think that Stephen is right, we should continue to publish more difficult angst-filled novels and complex biographies if they are so good they must be published. I think we editors and authors need to admit that we actually do wish to communicate with our readers. In turn, we need to have the confidence that a challenging, or quiet, or subtle YA book may be an important read, for the right reader. We need to climb down from the disdain and arrogance of pretending the needs of our readership do not matter, but we also need to challenge our readers to move past what is easy and appealing to what is truly distinguished. And the only way we

can do that is if the surrounding world takes such books as seriously as it once did *Goodnight Moon.*

To answer my title question, why publish so much angst if
teenagers don't want to read it? I answer, we *should* publish more
of the kinds of books teenagers want to read, especially humor.
But no simple sample of readers will tell us what kinds of books
those would be. After all, there are teenage readers who enjoy
angst and tears. And when a book is exceptional, we have the obligation to publish it and then do our best to help teenagers to understand why it matters.

As is so often true in the world of YA reading and publishing,
apparently simple questions bring us back to the gaps in our
knowledge and flaws in our systems of communication. We
don't know our readers well enough. Few critics are willing to
treat books for teenagers as literature. Teenagers have little guidance about important new books they should read. The first step
in ending this state of unhappy mutual ignorance is for us to recognize that it is there. Then we can begin the fascinating process
of learning how to communicate across the generation gap to
teenagers who no longer believe that one exists.

Chapter 12

What Is a YA Book, Anyway?

I wrote this essay in response to a request from the Illinois Young Adult librarians. As in so many of the pieces I write, I respond as an editor and publisher, but also as an author and historian. This overlapping of roles makes me always an insider and outsider to the world of books for young readers, but, also, I suspect makes me similar to teenagers, who are insiders and outsiders to their family and the adult world they are entering.

One of the most difficult decisions an editor or publisher has to make is whether or not a particular manuscript really is for teenagers. This question is not mainly one of anxiety about curse words, tough situations, or bleak endings. These may enter into the equation, though almost always in the form of market questions, not moral ones. That is, a book may be much harder to sell because of some of these red-flag issues, but that does not mean it is a less worthy creation; it may simply be a work that house cannot publish. In a very few cases the staff themselves may have a concern about something in a text. But this is the true exception. The real problem in assessing what is, or what should be published as a book for teenagers is that almost anything at all fits that description.

Teenagers can be reached, moved, inspired, instructed by adult books and comic books, true children's books they read while babysitting, and the great works of great thinkers that they read in Advanced Placement classes. But what in this great expanse of reading truly is a book for teenagers, not just a book teenagers may get something out of reading? In my experience, librarians—though to an extent teachers, parents, even editors and authors—who work with teenagers generally fall into one of two camps. I'd like to take this opportunity to suggest both camps take a new step in their evaluation of YA reading materials.

One faction is the literary, English major, artistic group. Their fondest hope is that teenagers will develop a love of reading, by which they really mean reading fiction. Launched up the reading ladder by YA novels, young people will move on and up to the great classics, to Jane Austen or Tony Morrison, or Maxine Hong Kingston. The teenagers will then join that subset of the American population that loves literary and semiliterary novels. Adults of this persuasion generally are willing to fudge over or excuse language or situations that might disturb others, so long as the overall literary quality is, in their opinion, high enough.

The other faction is the morals, role models, life choices crowd. Their dream is that teenagers, who are looking for a path, for direction, for ideas to believe in and codes of behavior around which to structure their lives, will find answers in books. They see in books the chance to reach out to a teenager who may be confused, to inspire one who may be despairing, to give concrete advice to one who is seeking help. Books, then, will lead teenagers on past the frightening rapids of adolescence into a happier, more stable life. This kind of adult adviser is often more alarmed about the use of language and depiction of specific kinds of situations in books. And yet, books in which teenagers "speak out," often in very direct ways about very tough matters, appeal far more to this kind of adult than to the literary crowd.

The literary types are happy enough if the book has a "message," but that is secondary. The morals folks are glad if the story is told "well," but style matters less to them than what they consider substance.

I think we can move past both positions. Both groups want to contain teenagers within the bounds they have found rewarding, rather than respecting and encouraging the as yet unbound hungers of the teenagers. Reading should open teenagers past the markers adults accept. But the intriguing thing is, written words can do this not by echoing teenagers' existing interests, but by revealing to teenagers interests and passions they hardly know they have. Our goal should not be to channel teenagers' interests, but to expand them as wide as they can go.

First we need to open up what we mean by reading to include websites, game instructions, car manuals, and, most of all, magazines. Books are just a subset of teenagers' true reading environment. Instead of ignoring all of those materials that do not come bound with convenient Dewey listings, we must see them as opportunities. Teenagers like magazines, which generally have lively design, contemporary ideas and situations, and target a wide range of interests. At Carus Publishing, our two fastest growing subscription bases are for *Muse*, our moxie, inquisitive nonfiction magazine, and *Cicada*, our literary YA magazine.

Second we need to open up our own approach to reading. Art in its largest sense is, I believe, about transformation. The artist sees, hears, dreams, deduces something, and then is able to render that idea or emotion or character or situation in a way that makes it vivid to someone else. That is a tad simplistic, since the artist may deliberately not want his or her audience to recognize the original, or may want the static, the difficulty of really knowing and understanding someone else's experience, to be a part of the final creation. Still, the heart of art is transforming something the artist experiences, through a medium he or she controls, into a new but perhaps also recognizable experience for someone else.

Teenage is precisely the time when a person is having a whole set of new physical, emotional, intellectual experiences, and is trying to make sense of them. The teenager is transmuting from child into adult. Art is important to teenagers not because they will then become good art appreciators, but because molting, shucking off one skin, one self, and finding a new one, is what they are doing every day. Teenagers should be exposed to as many forms of literary art, fiction and nonfiction, as possible. If adults view their role not so much as building fans for new novels but as supplying a kind of magic balm, a transmuting potion, that most will not feel at all, some will feel as a mild pleasant sensation every so often, and a few others will find as a secret echo of their innermost self, then they will be on the right track.

The moral group is right about one thing, teenagers are examining their beliefs, their lifestyle, and looking for answers—emotional answers, relationship answers, but also philosophical, religious, moral answers. As with the art crowd, I urge the morals people to go further. Don't just try to pass on the preset conclusions we've settled for. Celebrate this hunger, this yearning, this beginning-of-the-quest sensation that hits some teenagers like a lightning bolt. They must surpass us, go further in their questioning than we have. If we try to end their search just as they begin it, we deprive the world of their curiosity, their passion, their commitment. Just as the art crowd has to risk encouraging readers to like materials they themselves do not appreciate, the moral folks need to trust teenagers to be seekers.

To return to the publishing dilemma, a YA book is one that offers art and ideas in a fashion that communicates especially well to teenagers. A book a teenager should read, is any book.

Section 5

BOY TROUBLES:
THE CHALLENGES OF
BEING A MALE READER

Chapter 13

✛

Why Adults
Can't Read Boy Readers

I was in Chicago's Midway airport the other day, which gave me a good opportunity to spy on the reading habits of the American public. In our little bay, waiting for the plane, there were many adults immersed in magazines, a few with best-sellers cracked open, a teenage girl eagerly flipping through the pages of a color-splashed, ad-filled, celebrity-dominated magazine that was "just for her." The most avid reader of all, though, was tucked away in back, where he could concentrate. This was a boy who looked to be eleven or twelve, and he was studying his book with a concentration I saw nowhere else. His book was *How to Catch Yellow-Fin Tuna*. Ironically, from the point of view of the children's and young adult world, because of what he was reading, that boy passionately learning from those dense, printed pages, is a nonreader.

Boy readers, not boy nonreaders, present a problem that is so fundamental to the industry that creates, publishes, and reviews books for younger readers that we hardly know it is there. The problem is not that boys do not wish to read, but that what they wish to read—what, in fact, they desperately yearn to read—is not what we prefer to publish. I see this with my own son, Sasha, who is about to turn two. Like so many of his peers, he is passionate about cars. From the minute he wakes up and asks if we will use the car today to the second when he finally falls asleep as I read him *My Car*, or *Trucks*, or *I Love Trucks*, he thinks about cars.

Notice the disjunction. He loves cars, and I placate him with trucks. We have discovered trucks in children's books—and videos. But for a boy like my son who would love to start with the diagram in *My Car* and move on to learning to identify the parts of a car, and to getting a sense of how a car works, there is almost nothing. While the percentage of Americans living on farms diminishes to zero, American children grow up with barnyards full of sheep, goats, cows, chickens, and rabbits all baaing, mooing, and clucking at them across endless numbers of illustrated pages. But they cannot find out how these amazingly cool machines that they see, ride in, and dream about every day actually work.

There is a direct link between my son's unrequited lust for car books and that preteen boy poring over his adult fishing–instruction manual. In between the two is something else I observed on the short vacation that preceded the plane flight home. We had just gone for a brief stay at Benton Harbor, on the shores of Lake Michigan. The water was icy, far too cold for even a dip, though Sasha minded much less than my wife or I did. But one day I saw a bronzed dad and two of his equally tanned sons run by, in and out of the water, throwing a stick ahead, and training their two dogs to fetch. It was great splashing fun, but also serious business as the father showed the sons how you instruct dogs.

The next day we saw the same family again, although this time they were moving up the beach in the opposite direction. One was in a kayak, the other hopped off a small sailboat and swam—swam!—to join his brother. Then, without a moment of discussion, they linked the boat to the kayak, and paddled ahead in perfect unison, dragging the boat with them.

Those two snapshots showed something of what growing up male is all about. It is developing physical mastery, first of yourself and your own body, and second of the world around you through your body. This was much clearer when boys were being trained for physical jobs on those same farms immortalized now only in books for children, or in mines, or on assembly lines. Today physical mastery is most likely to take place through digital means—which is exactly what boys rehearse endlessly in video games.

The key point that the children's book world misses is that physical mastery requires concentration, intelligence, and the accumulation of knowledge. It also may involve bravery, humility, nobility, and certainly discipline and self-mastery. Of course it is this combination of sound mind, sound body that nineteenth-century English boy books preached, based, I am sure on the values of the schoolmasters of Eton and Rugby and Harrow—as well as Groton, Exeter, and Andover. We have come to doubt that combination, seeing the sexual undertone in "self-mastery," the homoerotics of the schoolmasters, the cruelty of the schoolyard games. But in becoming wiser, or more cynical, we have lost sight of a key to male growth. We have forgotten the intelligence needed to take control of your body, and, through it, to shape the world.

I do not question that this is important for girls, too. But note that so many of the stages of physical development in girls that were once off limits have become commonplace. In endless numbers of girl books, protagonists wonder about the appearance, size, and shape of their breasts; they fear, and then notice the appearance of their periods; they kiss, masturbate, have sex, and cope with the consequences. In turn there are boy books in which erections, nocturnal emissions, kissing, masturbation, sex, and consequences are central to the plot. But it is harder to find books in which physical maturation is not primarily about sexuality, but rather about the ability to influence and control the world. Certainly teenagers are very alert to how they can influence others through their sexuality, but that is really only one subset of their experience.

We tend to confine this other consideration of physical growth and the world to books about sports or survival—which is why the generic answer to any question about "what will my son like to read?" is *Hatchet*. We as an industry are not thinking like boys. We are not identifying with the curiosity of that sportfishing boy

I saw in the airport. We are not thinking, what would I need to know if I wanted to learn how to use my arms and legs and hands and brain to do X. Our books should be filling in that blank, between the boy's desire to engage in the world, his growing capacity to do so, and his lack of information about how he can. Our books should be the dad who once-upon-a-time lifted up the hood and explained how it all worked, and how he kept the jalopy on the road. Dads can no longer do that, with their leased cars that can only be repaired by mechanics with computers. But books can.

There is a great gap between boy, and even teenage, experience and the adult books those eager readers must turn to in order to answer their questions about the world. That gap will almost never be filled by fiction, or poetry, or folktales—although many folktales did serve that function in the communities that originally told them. They passed on wisdom. Boys hunger for wisdom, about themselves, about the world, about life. Our books prefer story and imagination, over wisdom and knowledge. Perhaps this is testimony to the fact that the women who have long been the guardians of children's literature were frustrated about their ability to act in the world. Imagination seemed so much more hopeful than fact. But today women run many of the publishing companies, library systems, and review journals; women make the book-buying decisions for chain bookstores. Surely we no longer need to turn away from grim fact to hopeful fantasy.

I think we need a literature that gets inside the excitement of taking hold of the world with your own hands and gaining control of it, through simple machines and complex ones; through physical (which we slander as "brute") strength, and through mental calculation and computation; we need books that understand the grace of kayaking in rhythm with your brother on a cold lake.

Until we as adults recognize this gap in the literature we create, we will not be able to respond to the aching needs of boy readers. And because we will not recognize that need, we will continue to call those boys nonreaders. Some will continue to make their way to adult books and magazines. Many will give up and when they put down the sports section, and turn off the complex instruction page they have just downloaded, and stop picturing just how they would turn the boat slightly differently next time to catch the wind and not tip over, they will believe that they do not like reading and have no imagination. A very few will decide that they like reading so much, they might as well read what we give them until they are old enough to read what they choose. This is the landscape of boy reading we see today, and it is the creation of our own blindness.

Though I loved cars when I was a child, I took the third route; I read what was available and never learned how a car works. I hope that when Sasha is a teenager he can explain it all to me. It is my job to create the books that will make this possible.

Chapter 14

✛

"Woke Up, Got Out of Bed, Dragged a Comb across My Head": Is the Past Knowable?

Written for a conference on children's literature and history, this essay in a sense extends the argument that I made in talking about boys on nonfiction. In order to understand what nonfiction for young readers should be I explore the resistance to it.

Hello everyone, thank you for inviting me to come to this conference on children's literature and history. This is a topic that I have cared about ever since the very first book I read by myself was a biography of George Washington. In a sense, to me, children's literature was American history. But as I came to work in the field, I found that children's literature and nonfiction in general had parted ways.

One reason for this divorce is a reigning anxiety about how to treat and evaluate nonfiction. What makes a nonfiction book "good"; how can we know if it is "accurate"? Theories about the past are often contentious—my "discovery" is your "conquest." How can we be sure an author is being objective? Some authors seem to try to deflect any criticism and produce dull, encyclopedic texts. Nonfiction for kids has been a kind of neglected stepchild, relegated to being "good for reports" and not generally considered great literature. Right here we can begin to answer these questions and determine what makes a good nonfiction book, or at least a good history book, which is a start.

Let's begin with an exercise. I'd like every one of you to think about what you did this morning, from the moment when you woke up until you got here. That should be relatively clear in your mind. If something dramatic had taken place during those hours, a robbery, a murder, an accident, and you had to account for your time in a court of law, it would be easy for you to find evidence to back up your memories. Witnesses are alive and available; you have credit card records for purchases; e-mails can be tracked, etc. Similarly, if some world historical event such as a plane flying into the World Trade Center occurred and you were asked "Where were you when you heard?" the moment would surely remain vivid in your memory, and you would have plenty of details to share.

Now think of this same morning as you will look back on it in five years or ten years. Surely some of that precision will have faded. It may well begin to blur into typical July mornings, or mornings before you came to conference sessions. Or you may weigh parts of the morning differently, realizing in retrospect what was "really" going on. Jump ahead, say, fifty years, and surely this morning that is so clear to you now will lose definition, and some of the evidence which could support or jog your memory will be lost.

If historians were interested in describing this morning, their ability to do so would depend on how much of that evidence survived, their general knowledge of this period, and their ability to make accurate, informed guesses. The first historian to write about this July morning might well rely on what each of you recall, which would have the value of being your own words, your own memories. A second, more skeptical writer might contrast your memories with surviving records, showing how you were imprecise, or self-serving, or mingling memory and myth. A third might find this quibbling over details fruitless, and focus instead on how you chose to describe your memories, suggesting that the real significance of this morning was not apparent even to you. Perhaps this morning was really only important as an instant in the environmental degradation of the planet, or the triumph of globalization, and any details of your car rides and cappuccinos would have to be seen as footnotes to that grand arc. But then a fourth historian might blend the surviving accounts to create a vivid and believable narration of the morning that readers could easily picture, and relive. While a fifth would argue that there is no single account of this morning, and rather the various stories, the ones you've told and those that historians have constructed, and that readers invent, are layered on top of each other, without end. And then finally a sixth researcher, perhaps the most rigorous of all, will only be willing to map what is known and unknown, knowable and not knowable, leaving us with fragments of a morning, but no clear and final picture.

If you considered each of these narratives as a kind of picture, the first would be a nostalgic nineteenth-century genre painting; the second a collage with romantic and realistic elements; the third a cubist abstraction or dissection of the scene; the fourth a modern neorealist mural or a history film; the fifth a postmodern juxtaposition of images that could even be an installation with flickering film images splashing over paintings and posters; the sixth might take original photos from this morning and show how they have faded, so that only parts are still visible.

I bet that if any of us went to a museum that featured those six different images of today, we would have some confidence about how to make sense of them. The same is not true of six different books about the past.

When we write about history for young readers, we enter at some point closer or further from the original events, depending on what topic we have chosen. What, then, is our obligation to our readers, and to the past? I think a great confusion has arisen because of the indeterminacy of the layering process. Because we have to acknowledge that there are many different accounts of the past, too many people throw up their hands and say, "It is all a matter of interpretation." I have my history, you have yours. In reverse, others may then want to ensure that young readers get only the facts, only what is certifiably true.

If you think about the example I gave you, your own history, it is obvious that neither of those answers make sense. Something did take place this morning. Or, to put it in reverse, it is possible to say things about what you did this morning that are not true. There are fictions about this morning, and truths. You did not meet a UFO, or slay a dragon, or see Elvis. So it is not all a matter of interpretation. On the other hand, as you go through life you do look back on events and view them in new lights. It is perfectly possible that, five, or ten, or certainly fifty years from now you will reinterpret this morning and realize that what you thought was minor, was crucial, or vice versa.

Real events take place, and then human beings interpret them. History is both the effort to recover those events, and the play of mind as we try to make sense of ourselves through the semireflective mirror of the past. One of the great joys for me when I begin working on a new book, such as the one on the seventeenth-century Puritans that I have just finished, is to read the historiography of that period. I not only get to discover what we know about people and events, but also to look at the sequence of theories, schools, ideas about that time.

Reading through books on the Puritans in Massachusetts and in England during the period of its civil war, I had the curious experience of passing through layers of assumptions about "what every schoolchild knows." Authors would refer to stories, such as when John Winthrop wrote his "A Model of Christian Charity" on board the *Arbella*, or Captain John Endicott cut the cross of St. George out of the English flag, or Oliver Cromwell won the battle of Marston Moor, as events that were so familiar it was hardly necessary to describe them again. Obviously any reader would have encountered these central moments in grade school. But we no longer treat our history as so directly connected to that of England, nor that of Massachusetts. "What every schoolchild knows" about these events is absolutely nothing.

What should they know? In the old books there was a heroic arc to the story: American freedom was born in England and flowered here. Historians have dismantled that simple narrative. Now many focus on the religious passions of the time, the sense in which both Winthrop and Cromwell truly believed that they were at the end of time, that the ultimate battle between good and evil had started, and that Jesus would return very soon. In the wake of the September 11th attacks, I found that new view all the more fascinating. The leaders who helped to establish New England had a great deal in common with the modern Taliban. And yet some also, eventually, came to support religious toleration and a kind of democracy and freedom of speech. The shift in our view of the seventeenth century does not make it less relevant to today. Just the opposite, it makes it a mirror of our time. But an author can only learn this by comparing one history book against another, studying how historians' views change over time. That is what makes historical research so interesting.

I do not find that my joy is shared in the children's book world. Parents, teachers, librarians, even authors, want a clear answer. What happened, which view can we trust, what is true? Burned by the culture wars and intimidated by militant guardians of "accuracy," adults want to be sure they have not offended, have not slipped, have not gotten it wrong. Or, they think that the history itself will not be of interest to young readers, and so they have to "get creative," fictionalize it, make it into a story. I think the creativity is inherently there, in the effort to make sense of the past.

I have just completed a second book about the seventeenth century, *Witch-Hunt*, and it is about the Salem witch trials. Why were nineteen people executed in Salem in 1692? Why did a group of accusers, mainly teenage girls but also including adult men and women, experience or fake symptoms in court that convinced panels of judges that evil spirits were loose right there and then? Why did the courts, which before and after this outbreak most often found those accused of witchcraft not guilty, change their standards? Why did the leading ministers of Massachusetts indicate, from the first, that they had doubts about the trials, but not campaign to bring them to an end? We simply do not know. We do know that medical or biological explanations, such as that the symptoms were caused by eating rotten wheat, are highly unlikely. And the historian Mary Beth Norton has just published a fascinating new study that gives us new insights into the judges. But as we cannot answer the most basic question—

were the accusers consciously lying, and if so why?—we have no way to evaluate exactly what they experienced in court.

Salem is ultimately a mystery. But that does not make it any less interesting. It is interesting to describe what we know of what took place. It is interesting to look back at all the theories about those events and try to evaluate them. It is interesting to try to look past what we know to see how we might learn more. It is satisfying to give young readers a road map to the evidence and theories, so they can build their own investigations on a solid foundation.

The very uncertainty over the basic matter of guilt and responsibility invites teenagers to enter into the debate. Were the accusers a pack gone mad with the power to destroy or were they individuals already in a crazed, hysterical state who could no longer separate their nightmares and their daily lives? Many of the accusers were teenagers, and it seems to me that once we give modern teenagers enough historical context to ground their judgments, their psychological insights are likely to be perceptive. And even if their speculations are wrong, I am convinced that trying to puzzle out this mystery will fascinate many teenagers. I do not need to fictionalize the intensely dramatic events of the pretrial hearing or simplify the problems in evaluating evidence in order to make the testimony vivid. I simply have to invite teenagers into the process of thinking about the words they read.

And yet, as I described in chapter eight, it is also true that one of the great works of historical fiction, Arthur Miller's *The Crucible,* was written about the trials. That is what historical fiction can do, re-create events in a way that feels compelling, that tells what seem to be basic or essential truths of the human condition. Historical novels are new creations built out of an admixture of materials of the past and present. Creative nonfiction is also an amalgam of present insight and past artifact, and surely all history also reflects the time in which it was written and the conscious or unconscious drives of the author. But there is a crucial difference between the two forms. In historical fiction the author's first obligation is to be engaging, moving, lively, revealing, insightful. In creative nonfiction the author's first obligation is not to be false.

This is why I simply cannot see why any author would not supply notes allowing readers to see where he or she got information. You owe it to your reader to show your hand, so the reader can follow your trail, see if you got it right, see what sources you did or did not use. You cannot pretend to be omniscient. If you were an engaged, thoughtful, resourceful researcher, that journey is part of what you have to share with your young readers.

I hear your objections: what you are saying sounds fine for academic or adult books, but what good is it to write for young readers if they will not read what you write? Aren't you as obligated to be engaging, moving, lively, revealing, insightful in nonfiction for kids as in fiction? Isn't the reason for calling something a book for younger readers the fact that you have those readers in mind and have aimed your text towards them? If that is so, why add notes to the back that very few of them will read?

Writing for younger readers does make special demands on us, primarily that we communicate well with them. But that does not imply that we have to write only fiction. I really do think that a good part of that belief comes because too many people who judge children's literature prefer fiction, and so assume this is true of all readers. They forget how pleasing it is to a young reader to discover a fact, not just a gross-out fact, or a fun fact, or a factoid, but a bit of new knowledge about the universe.

I often hear people complain that their history teachers made them memorize facts. I am sure that there are terrible history teachers in the world, and that this dry emphasis on fact was frustrating for some. But learning facts can also be exciting. Many young people are very proud to be able to name the presidents in order. It is cool when you know what the Gadsen Purchase was, or what "54/40 or Fight" meant, or how much Seward paid for Alaska. This is certainly not all that history has to offer. But I think that English majors who especially dislike these kinds of nonnarrative names and dates tend to write the novels and memoirs that establish our image of childhood. In the children's literature world we rarely hear from the grown-ups who as kids loved memorizing facts.

Our critics also forget how excited teenage readers can be to discover new ideas, new theories about themselves, the world, politics, society, the meaning of existence. They forget that biography offers young people not just role models, but unique, complex examples of what it is to be a human being. Facts, ideas, biographies do not need to be fictionalized to be fascinating.

It is true, though, that very often books of facts, biographies, textbooks, tend to be dull. And I wonder if this may not be a reflection of our uncertainty as adults. We are not entirely sure what young readers know or need to know about a topic. This makes us say too much or too little. We pause to define too many words—or provide boxes and sidebars to fill in gaps—or we shrink what we have to say down to the simplest, most digestible form. We also lack the confidence in our storytelling abilities that someone like Hendrick Van Loon possessed. One feels that he was sure he could describe anything in an engaging fashion, and so it was no problem for him to tackle an entire history of the world.

Our anxiety is fed by the flood of information, theories, ideas circulating in the adult world. Even a well-educated person no longer expects to really understand how his computer works, or the human genome project, or the latest theories about how the universe actually exists in eleven dimensions, most of which are folded in on themselves. We are overwhelmed with bits of knowledge, or an awareness that there is knowledge out there to be had, but which we do not possess. Where do we begin, or end, in telling young readers about the world when we cannot sort that out for ourselves?

The fact that we all loyally ask experts to review our books on fossils and tigers and space flight is not just a sign of our sense of responsibility. It is also a kind of admission of defeat: knowledge belongs to experts; we are only amateurs struggling to pass along a comprehensible bit to kids. We don't expect to know enough ourselves to get it right. We lack the confident gusto of an earlier era. Think of, say, a granddad explaining how to make a special fishing lure, or an uncle pointing here and there as he tinkers with his ancient car to keep it on the road, or a neighbor with a sure hand showing how to sew and quilt. None of those people needed to consult experts. Our nonfiction has none of the cozy confidence any of these people had, or have.

I say this because when you think of those examples of personal transmission, nonfiction for kids has the least chance of being dull. Young people are eager to know new things, fascinated with discoveries large and small, hungry to make the world around them their own. Fiction requires us to invent it, and we may not be talented at that. Nonfiction is simply giving kids what they want and need. It is offering a kind of basic sustenance that they crave.

Perhaps the key to meeting this need lies in seeing ourselves as partners in discovery with our readers. We don't know enough when we set out to write our books. Our readers do not know what they will find when they open our pages. We both start out with curiosity, a desire to know. We need not know it all. Instead, let us use what we do know, which is how to communicate, and share our process of discovery with our readers. One of the great nonfiction series for younger readers is called *Let's Read and Find Out*. I say we take that one step further: together, I as adult author, and you as young reader, will find out together. I will share the process of discovery, not just its end.

Nonfiction that can have this humility and freshness will not be dull. It will have the point-and-click openness of online searches with the narrative control of a book. Let me give you one final example of how this works. Susan Kucklin is an excellent author and photographer who has written over thirty books for young readers. But in only one of them, a book we did together called *Trial*, did she include herself in the story. The book tells young people about how the law works, by following a kidnapping case in New York from beginning to end. As she interviewed lawyers, defendants, and—after the trial—jurors, Susan was learning. She was not an omniscient narrator, she was a kind of student. Just a few weeks ago she presented the book to 120 eighth graders in the South Bronx, a notoriously poor and neglected part of the city.

Every single one of them had read it, and they responded enthusiastically to meeting her. None of the issues we are taught to worry about—difficult concepts, long words, unfamiliar terms bothered them. Instead, they were glad to learn. The attitude that Susan had in creating the book communicated directly to her readers. That is the key to making nonfiction work, not inventing stories or characters, hiding notes, using simple words, nor filling pages with sidebars.

All of these themes about nonfiction, history, and books for younger readers come together when you think of teenagers. It is both the nature and the necessity of teenagers to be eager and cynical, wide-open as at no other time of life, and filled with half-formed and passionately held judgments. No one needs new ideas, new information, new depth of understanding as much as a teenager, and no one is more likely to dismiss what she finds as useless, irrelevant, and dull than a teenager. No one has greater need to understanding the laws, rules, traditions, and history of the world he is entering than a teenager, and no one is more likely to disregard anything outside of his present world.

The teenager is, also, flooded with information in school. Not only do we have to compete for the teenager's attention against popular culture, we need to convince him or her to pay attention to us after wading through endless textbook pages and homework assignments.

It seems to me our only chance of accomplishing this is to appeal to their interest in thinking. As a contrast to the predigested and carefully manicured world of the textbook, we need to offer the questioning, searching mind of a teenager our own theories, uncertainties, and debates. Unlike the prepackaged glitz of popular culture, we need to show teenagers the true depth and complexity of research, scholarship, and open-ended inquiry. We need to use our books to invite teenagers to become adults not simply by learning to mimic the right answers on tests or by participating in mass-produced culture but by thinking for themselves. Our only chance of doing that *for* them is by doing it *with* them.

I set out this goal for teenage nonfiction because it sets a tone for everything we do. If the aim of nonfiction for young readers is to prepare them for this last stage, this stage of thinking and questioning, then that is what we should be doing all along. Instead of assuming that we need to turn to fiction to smooth and ease the way; instead of hiding our confusion by getting experts to agree that our précis look more or less right, or at least not wrong, we should treat nonfiction as a craft that is as personal as novel writing. A book is a path an author has taken in search of knowledge. It is the journal, the record, of that search, as well as the reward for undertaking the journey. If we approach nonfiction for younger readers in this way it will have the excitement of the adventure story, the inspiration of the quest, the drama of the pathway into the unknown, and the unique satisfaction of offering those readers nuggets of insight that allow them to understand the world around them. This is a high calling and as long as we keep it in mind, nonfiction, instead of being the stepchild of our literature, will take its rightful place as its glory.

Section 6

BACK TO PARTICULARS
AND UNIVERSALS

Chapter 15

Am I My Brother's Keeper?

This, the last talk I gave while working on this book, is also a fitting conclusion to it. I explore the theme of brotherhood in the recent history of books for adults and children, at the same time I look at how the implicit relationship of the reader to the family changes as a child grows. The two are linked, for they have to do with how we envision the family, the reader, and the role of books. In which ways is a child embedded in surrounding circles such as home, school, ethnic group, nation? How does the individual sensibility of the young reader interact with these group pressures, and with the individual sensibility of the author? Responding to these questions returns me to the themes I discussed in the introduction: the one and the many, the individual and the group.

The attacks on 9/11 were the clearest expression of an assault on America as a collectivity—they assaulted all of us. But they were also undertaken in the name of an ideology that saw us as too individualistic compared to the Islamic sense of brotherhood. It was the tension between these two senses of self and community I explored in the two essays on the Puritans. Now a bit further removed in time from the attacks, I feel less urgency to find a ground in the past, in understanding. But the same basic sense is behind this piece: our literature must help young people to see themselves as part of a larger world, and to see themselves apart

from that world—learn from others and *think for yourself, study* and
create, understand and *invent.*

*I suppose, as this piece shows, those themes hearken back to my own
childhood, to the progressive education I experienced. I see many flaws
in that approach now, but looking back at the objectives of those educa-
tors as I define them here, and forward to this collection, there is a direct
link in the sense of internationalism, the vision of interracialism not defined by ethnic separation, and the belief in critical thinking. What you
learn young does influence you, even in questioning what you learned.*

I am grateful, if a bit intimidated, by this opportunity to think
out loud with the elite company of children's book readers,
critics, creators, and advocates that is Children's Literature
New England. I have heard tales of the care with which Virginia Euwer Woolf selected her words to share with you, and
that sets a very high mark to aim at. I was not even entirely
sure which topic to tackle. But then something in the conference's theme touched on a strand in my thinking that has been
especially important to me this year. "Am I my brother's
keeper?" How can we begin to answer that within the universe
of children's literature? It seemed to me that that classic question actually contained within it an unstated but central problem, and until that is addressed the overall issue is so broad as
to be meaningless.

The answer to this question depends entirely on what you
mean by "brother." Is "brotherhood" a relationship of blood or
adoption defined by birth or legal status? Is it a sign of membership in a particular ethnic, social, religious, or even gender
group? In that sense, is fraternity exactly the same as sorority? Is
it about being part of a peer group, or some other cluster or
clique you qualify to join such as the Elks, Rotarians, the Brotherhood of Sleeping Car Porters, or even Skull and Bones? Or is
it a broader term implying membership in the global human
family?

Once you start to look at the word you see that "brotherhood"
can have many varied and even diametrically opposed meanings, and each of these has its own implication for the kind of

fraternal responsibility the relationship mandates. "Brother-hood" can be almost flaccidly inclusive, used in that sense to erase any sense of difference among competing nations and peoples. Or it can be specifically exclusive, suggesting a bond among one set of people unique to them that defines them as different from others.

Even in the simplest and strictest sense, that of being a sibling, the term pulls in opposite directions. In the obvious Hallmark sense, it implies a baseline affection that endures all of life's changes. A brother is an ally whose allegiance is a condition, not an arrangement. "He ain't heavy, he's my brother." But even the shallowest sense of psychology tells us that the bond is as much formed in the darker regions of competition and comparison where the sibling is the rival as in the sunny lands of camaraderie and companionship. It was Cain, after all, who first posed the question as a defiant response to God, just after he murdered Abel. "What's it to me," he was saying, "everybody better look out for himself in this tough world."

All of these meanings of "brother" are especially relevant to us in the world of literature for younger readers. By definition our readers are embedded in some kind of family, they are children—I'll get to teenagers a bit later on. How we define "brother" says a great deal about how we define that family. And, I will argue, the many ambiguities about the meanings of "brother" both map out key categories within the literature we create and study, and help us to see the conflicts and changes that are rumbling within and around those books. Let's explore some of the implications of the books we and the surrounding adult world have produced, and see how they lead us back to our original question about sibling obligation and responsibility.

The classic adult book that took the broadest view of brother-hood is *The Family of Man*. As Edward Steichen, the photographer who organized the 1955 exhibit that gave rise to the book, explained, it "was conceived as a mirror of the universal elements and emotions in the everydayness of life—as a mirror of the essential oneness of mankind throughout the world." "*The Family of Man*," he concluded, "has been created in a passionate spirit of devoted love and faith in man." Carl Sandberg's resounding Whitmanesque prologue ended with this affirmation:

> There is only one man in the world
> And his name is All Men.
> There is only one woman in the world
> And her name is All Women
> There is only one child in the world
> And the child's name is All Children.

There is a nearly uncountable strand of children's books, from picture books through library reference books, from folktales and novels through series on nations, peoples, and cultures throughout the world that shares this view of childhood. Just casually walking through the exhibit hall at a recent American Library Association conference I came across many examples of this sort of book from publishers such as National Geographic, and in a related but only slightly different vein, Susan Kuklin's *Walls*.

Like *The Family of Man* itself, these books are often well-produced, photographically driven, and aim at inspiring a sense of wonder at the intriguing differences that crop up within our essential oneness. They take what might be called an anthropological or, if you are so inclined, semi-Jungian, Levi-Straussian, structuralist view of culture and psychology. They encourage self-absorbed children to see their similarity with others near and far, while enticing the curious to become aware of our fascinating diversity.

Such books answer our frame question with a kindhearted and urgent advocacy, which is also often combined with an ecological message: "All people are your brothers and sisters; together we must honor and protect our mother earth." To make this exact point, *The Family of Man* used many quotations from indigenous peoples, such as this Sioux prayer: "With all beings and all things we shall be as relatives." This is, of course, the message of the entire library of what might be called *Brother Eagle, Sister Sky* books.

Above and beyond even these broad categories of children's books, this universalized sense of brotherhood and childhood was the basis of the international organizations for children and their literature, such as International Board on Books for Young

People (IBBY) and UNESCO. And this view achieved a lasting political expression in the UN Declaration on the Rights of the Child, which was itself then made into a children's book. It is, or, more accurately, was, the foundation of any sense of internationalism in our sense of childhood.

I grew up being entranced by the Richard Halliburton books, became a children's book editor by working on the Land and People books, the Portraits of the Nations series. I've served on the board of United States Board on Books for Young People and am proud to have edited two books that won the Batchelder Prize and one Batchelder Honor book, so I certainly share something of this point of view. But, as my long-suffering aunt Cheyna—who had lived through the Russian Revolution, two world wars, and was married to a Yiddishist who lived across the street from Columbia University but refused to learn English—used to say, "it is not so simple."

The Family of Man was not just created as an affirmation, but as a warning. It was a portrait of universalism designed to prevent the destruction of humanity. It was an homage to sight—to the clarity and understanding that could come through photos—that was deliberately blind. Thirteen pages from the end of the book on a completely black page in drop-out white type, Bertrand Russell warns that "a war with hydrogen bombs is quite likely to put an end to the human race." Steichen was careful to include photos from throughout the world, from both sides of the then Iron Curtain. By making his themes the stages of life, from love, to sex, to birth, to family, work, play, marriage, death, faith, he also very carefully avoided anything that marked differences among nations and ideologies. "If we could only see what we have in common," the book seems to plead, "we would never consider destroying each other."

In *The Family of Man*, there were no Communists preaching world revolution, freedom fighters trying to liberate their nations, or NATO forces drilling soldiers or building bombs. And remember that 1955 was the year of the suppressed uprising in Hungary. There were no segregationists or Klan rallies, no Civil Rights protestors. And recall that this was the year of the Montgomery bus boycott. There were no atheists fighting to keep church and state separate and no fundamentalists demanding that "under God" be inserted into the Pledge of Allegiance, as it had been just the year before. So many of the issues that now seem crucial to the mid-fifties could not be in a book that tried to heal by ignoring conflict.

This is precisely the approach that the Cold War mandated for organizations such as IBBY. Children were great. Childhood was great. Books for children were great. But no one was allowed to raise any issues about the beliefs and opinions those children were likely to have as adults. The damaging consequence of this approach can be seen in the later history of so many UN departments: while their rhetoric became ever more inclusive, the actual organizations were scenes of the most callous and calculated maneuvering among political blocks. The paradigmatic outcome of this mixture of naïveté and cynicism was the conference on racism that took place in Durban just before the outbreak of the latest *Intifada* in the Middle East.

Though the threat of nuclear war these days seems either a regional concern in the subcontinent or a particularly horrifying form of domestic terrorism, not a global issue, I think that an implicit threat is still the shadow behind books of this sort. Whether their message is internationalism, the protection of endangered species, or a broader sense of ecology and global citizenship, there is a kind preaching that always implies that if we do not get the good message we will be faced with bad consequences. "We had best be our brothers' keepers, or we shall all be as Cain, casting destruction and evil across the land."

This bland sense of sharing is also coercive, for by not mentioning difference and conflict, it implies that such things are not to be discussed. The need for the whole to work together is far greater than for individuals to air their confusions. Perhaps it is this do-gooder quality combined with hidden coercion that confines many books that take this approach to the younger ages. The books are like a certain brand of nursery school teacher who is wonderful at encouraging good attitudes in kids, but also something of a tyrant.

History, though, is important here, because it suggests that the time has come to reconsider this particular brand of internationalism in children's literature. This comfort in vague universals and avoidance of prickly particulars was not only a product of international Cold War pressures, but also domestic ones. Some years ago at a historians' conference I met Julia Mickenberg, now an American studies professor at the University of Texas at Austin. She alerted me to a subtheme she had uncovered in her research on children's literature and the Left in the forties and fifties: some Communist and strongly left authors and illustrators who feared being blacklisted found a home in children's books. She found three themes in children's books that were a translated expression of this merger of the ideals of progressive education and left politics: a focus on interracial understanding and against prejudice, an emphasis on realism and science, and an advocacy of critical thinking.

Here's just one particularly apt example of how politics and the arts blended and made their way into kids' books. In 1947, a group of radical and left-wing cartoonists created a feature called *The Brotherhood of Man*. Based on the research of the famous anthropologist Ruth Benedict and her Columbia colleague Gene Weltfish, it used animation to play with and meld peoples' skin tones and racial characteristics. Working against this image of multiracial commonality was the figure of suspicion, a little green, curmudgeonly man. One of the authors of the script was a very talented and politically committed animator named John Hubley. According to the historian Michael Denning, Hubley went on to become the main creator of Mr. Magoo, who seems to have been based on the suspicious green man, and Hubley's art style and satiric sense of humor were important influences on Gerald McBoing Boing. Magoo and McBoing Boing were expressly designed to be unlike Disney or Warner Brothers cartoons, and both, of course, made their way into children's books—some of my favorite books when I was a child, I might add.

I am not saying that Magoo or McBoing Boing need to be analyzed for hidden messages. Nor, especially, that they were created to corrupt kids and subtly turn them into commies. But I do think that it would be useful to examine children's books of the postwar period in light of the brand of internationalism and ethos of commonality of peoples that arose in consciously left circles in the depression and forties. It would make those positions historical, not simply universal and eternal. And it would lead us, living in a time of a very different kind of globalism, to rethink how to portray this baseline sense of our common humanity. Today we are joined in what we buy and sell, not in what we build, mine, and manufacture. It is the solidarity of merchants, not laborers, that now links the globe.

The first meaning of brotherhood, then, is most frequently seen in books for younger children, and leans toward a bland yet coercive universalism that was a product of both the Cold War and the McCarthy blacklist. I have an alternate image of globalism to propose that is more relevant to the world of open markets, selfinterest, and borderless commerce that is characteristic of our world today.

I had the good fortune to be in Washington for the opening of the Silk Road festival at the national mall. It was fascinating for me to get to see the photos I published in Land and People books come to life, the dances I occasionally saw on grainy newsreels about life in the Soviet Union in full color right in front of the Washington Monument. The Silk Road is an image we might look at for a new sense of internationalism and brotherhood. It is about commerce, not ideals; it is about exchanges among peoples who are different, but eager to learn and borrow; it finds our common humanity not in some universal All Men, All Women, All Children, but in the specific ways we adapt and change. We honor and protect our brothers because we want to keep the trade routes open and the exchanges flowing. We do not have to hide our differences, because difference is what gives us things to trade.

Professor Mickenberg's mention of the Left's devotion to overcoming racial bias leads to my second sense of brotherhood. For the Socialists, Communists, and humanitarian idealists of the thirties, forties, and fifties the universal identity of all human beings was a core belief. As against nativism, Fascism, Nazism, Father Caughlin, the Klan, the DAR, they spoke for what they called "the people."

The classic expression of this New Deal era belief was Earl Robinson's *Ballad for Americans*, which was recorded in 1940 by

Paul Robeson, assisted by the American People's Chorus—a group made up of working-class amateur singers. I grew up singing this too, so I hear the melodies with the lyrics as I read them: "I'm the everybody who's nobody. I'm the nobody who's everybody. I'm an engineer, musician, street cleaner, carpenter, teacher." The chorus adds, "farmer, office clerk, mechanic, housewife, factory worker, stenographer, beauty specialist, bartender, truck driver, ditch digger." Who are these many Americans ethnically? "I'm just an Irish, Negro, Jewish, Italian, French and Swedish, Finnish, Canadian, Greek and Turk, and Czech and double Czech American."

To counter any exclusionary sense of being American, Robeson and the ballad asserted that we were all, all-American. Though it is interesting that film stars, athletes, lawyers, business leaders—so many of the careers young people long for today—did not make the list. This was a vision of inclusiveness built out of common labor. And it was specifically this sensibility that welcomed authors such as Richard Wright, Langston Hughes, and Arna Bontemps, and artists such as Jacob Lawrence.

Let's look, then, by contrast, at Walter Dean Myers' *Brown Angels*. This lovely book proposes a different sense of brotherhood than that of the ballad. By culling images of black children from the many he has collected throughout his lifetime, matching them with his own poetry, and then displaying the pairings on handsomely designed pages meant to be reminiscent of a beloved family album, Myers is, I believe, making two kinds of claims. By beautifully displaying this treasure trove of images of black children, he is speaking to two distinct communities. He is saying to other African Americans, see how beautiful we are, see, in this family album, we as we know ourselves to be. As he puts it, "Black hearts, strong hearts, hearts beating on, Oh honor the memory!" At the same time he is asserting to others, those outside the African American world, that we are not the images of enslavement, suffering, frustration you see in the media. Our baby pictures are just like yours. Recognize our similarity by seeing us as we do in private.

A key link between these two agendas is that, because these are images of babies and children, they immediately make us think of family. In each image the book reminds us of the strength of the black family. Historians have debated the effect of slavery on that social unit. In the 1950s, most believed black family life suffered damage from which it still had not recovered. But by the sixties others suggested that an extended family system developed in which responsibilities were spread beyond parents who might be separated and sold. But Myers' book points beyond either of those positions. It says that, whatever its nature, family life is at the center of black life. And by making that statement, he both challenges stereotypes and builds bridges. That is the glory of this book.

While the implicit theme of *Brown Angels* is of a shared humanity, that image is transmitted by portraying a distinct and separate community. Here is a brotherhood defined by race that offers a more inclusive vision only by equating one group with another. Instead of "the nobody who is everybody," instead of "one child who is all children" we have black children who collectively are a kind of single child, made thus the same—or, more accurately, different in detail but cute, sweet, entrancing in the same ways as all white, or all Asian, or all Indian children. The equivalences are between and among groups.

This shift from the brotherhood of labor, of "the people" to the brotherhood of distinct ethnic groups took place, of course, from the late sixties on as the Left divided over Black Power. Soon more and more people were eager to reconnect to their own roots, whether in Jewish neo-orthodoxy or Celtic music. In many respects I think this was a needed advance. American history has been most significantly binary, black and Anglo-Saxon white—with all other versions of humanity sometimes collapsed into black, as, say, was often the case for Asian or Indian, or sometimes into white, as became the case for Italian and Jewish after World War II. It was this fundamental fact that everyone, from the radicals of the sixties through authors such as Walter Dean Myers, urged us to recognize and to face.

There was a healthy realism to this acknowledgment of racism. It was as if we as a nation were leaving childhood with its do-gooder tyrant teachers and entering a more raucous middle school and junior high. Battles were more out in the open. Asserting that a white person could never get a black character right was a clear statement that the old brotherhood of universals had been discarded as a fiction useful only for little ones. In the rough and tumble of the new world, each group would speak for itself. Brotherhood had first to be found within each group, and then among groups. Until the basic inequalities in American life that predetermined how black kids would be judged were addressed, it was silly to speak of a more general sense of fraternity and responsibility.

But that moment of racial realism, and racial solidarity, was just as much a product of history as was *Ballad for Americans*. And I believe that moment, too, has passed. It is interesting that, this year, two books on Woody Guthrie, who was clearly a champion of the older version of what it meant to say "This Land Belongs to You and Me," have been honored by the Boston Globe Horn Book committees, and that in recent surveys more and more young people prefer to define themselves as American, rather than any particular ethnic group. Now it could be that the young people are expressing a nativist sentiment, a rejection of hyphenation. But they may also be expressing a yearning to get beyond the distinctness and separation of definition by group, by ethnicity, and searching for a broader definition in which a great variety of cultural and ethnic and racial influences are assumed to have shaped all of us.

One reason for this may be the remarkable increase in interracial marriages, and now interracial children. As Pearl Gaskins showed in her book of interviews with mixed-race teenagers and college students, *What Are You?* being forced to choose being black or Korean, Jewish or Chinese, meant being false. These young people know in their genes, in the faces they see in their mirrors, in their family photos, that brotherhood cannot be established by groups. Mixture is the ever-more-obvious condition of our lives. If the Silk Road is the image that I think should replace *The Family of Man*, the mixed child is the next step beyond *Brown Angels*.

Mixture is not the same as muddying; it does not mean pretending there are no difficulties, no conflicts. Rather it is saying that we can contain within each of ourselves more than one heritage, more than one ethnicity, more than one set of affinities. We can be both; we need not lose either. Brothers are distinct individuals, but within the same family. Our mixed children will be carrying within themselves two brothers, each of their lineages, and the challenge of being a good sibling will take place internally as well as externally. "Am I the keeper of that other tradition, that other heritage, that is also part of me?"

We now come to yet a third meaning of brotherhood that has arisen recently in adult and children's books. This can be found in photographic books that show images of sisters, or mothers and daughters, or twins. The images are meant to be heartwarming, reminding us of family bonds and individual differences, of change within continuity. Each book is designed to be a perfect gift, a way to say to your sibling, we are as bonded as they are, joined not just by genes but heart to heart.

The familial sense of sisterhood is as much a staple of middle-grade children's books as the eco-message books are of childhood. From the coping books helping an older sibling to accept the arrival of a new family member through endless books on friendships turned sour as an older sister becomes a teenager, this is familiar territory. Too much so. Looking back at folktales and out at the new America that is emerging in the new era of immigration, we can see what is missing. And this links back to the old debates over the black family.

I think our sense of the sibling relationship is both too shallow and too narrow. Recently my wife Marina was reading a collection of Indian folktales. Over and over in stories about sisters she saw a similar pattern, one that we know best in plays such as King Lear. Within the family one sister was going to win, and another was going to lose. One would win the prince, would get the dowry, would be honored by her parents, and another would be cast out, would have to make do with scraps, in most cases was actually killed, and even eaten up. Often the story is about a reverse, where the loser is kind to a snake or some other magical creature, and returns in glory. The Puritan version of exactly such tales shows up in the records of witch trial hearings, where a poor girl who has lost out in the family struggle is tempted by a voice she hears from the air, or from an animal, or in her mind. A voice that offers all she desires, if she will only sign the black book with her red blood.

The intensity of these stories is in part a testimony to inheritance laws and dowry customs. Siblings were not just in competition over affection, but literally over the property that would define their futures. That is not so much the case anymore. But I think our fiction settles for cute, for temperamental, for eccentric in dealing with sibling relations and avoids the darker territory that folktales are more honest about. Cain's fury at Abel is not over land, it is over love: whose offerings are accepted by God, by the father. Who is the favored child? And what can the rejected sibling do with his consuming rage and envy? If our literature is to answer Cain's question, it must look into his heart.

Our literature of the family should look down deeper, and it must also look out. What is the sibling family relation? Today in more and more families, the sibling is a hybrid. This is so in blended families, in families with a mix of blood and adoptive children, and in families that are embedded in a larger web of relations. Just as the extended family reared black children during slavery, many new immigrants arriving in America do not limit their sense of the sibling to the children of one set of parents. Recently a friend of Marina's invited her to become a cousin-sister, as are so many other women in her Indian family. Aunties in the subcontinent are not necessarily defined by blood at all. They are, a bit like yentas in the Jewish context, women who are involved, if a bit overinvolved, in your life.

I think a whole literature will soon emerge in which a growing child's sister is a cousin, her auntie is not a relative, her stepbrother is her idol, and her own is an enemy. In other words, the sibling relationship exists, but is spread out among all of the links that exist in many countries outside of the United States, and are becoming more and more important in childhood here. Am I my brother's keeper? Which brother do you mean? How will that question sound to the adopted Chinese daughter of the lesbian couple who also had a child through artificial insemination, and the father of that child has children the girl has gotten to know?

So far, most of the books I have discussed have been nonfiction. And that is deliberate. I think nonfiction does as good a job as fiction in creating a sense of brotherhood, and often it does it better. Fiction takes us inside a character or a situation, but it is the product of one person's insight, imagination, and skill. Nonfiction takes us out into the world, in all its complexity. Nonfiction levels us, as products of history, and connects us, showing the forces that influence us all. Fiction often inspires and rewards introspection. Nonfiction inspires and rewards curiosity. And curiosity is precisely what we need to connect to the rest of the world.

The last sense of brotherhood I want to consider, though, is mainly a matter of fiction. It helps us to understand one of the conundrums that exists in all of children's literature: how do YA novels, the books of teenage, link up to children's books? As I mentioned at the start, in all of the books we have been considering, the reader, the child is part of the family. The challenge of adolescence is to become an individual, to leave the family. I think it is this baseline difference that creates so much of the anxiety around YA literature.

Inasmuch as we—authors, publishers, reviewers, parents, librarians, teachers—want our books for younger readers to pass on our ideals and values, we feel a kind of queasiness about YA books. After twelve years or so of trying to get kids to listen to us through books, we have three years of trying to help them think for themselves. We just don't know how to connect those two opposite agendas.

Cain is speaking as a kind of prototypical teenager: *Look, Dad, we are not in that safe warm family anymore. You said that was over. You said once we disobeyed you, once we saw behind the platitudes and realized how the world really works, once we realized what sex was all about, you said we were on our own. I believed you, Dad, I was the good son. I got the cold, hard message of realism, of reality. We are all out for ourselves in this world. And if that soft, coddled brother of mine didn't, if he was still dreaming that you would protect him, that's his fault for staying a child when it was time to grow up. There are no brothers in this world, Dad. There are just individuals who know where their bread is buttered, what's good for each of them.*

It is precisely this sense of individuation that teenagers need to achieve in adolescence. But of course we hope that what we taught them in the earlier years will also kick in. We pray that they will bring something of the family with them when they venture out alone, and will bring back to the family something of what they discover on the way. We hope our teenage children are prodigals who come back, not Cains who are condemned to slink across the earth. The challenge of YA literature, I believe, is to give the reader freedom to roam so he can freely return, and yet enough help, enough inspiration, enough guidance and sense so that he or she has a compass on the path.

I faced a dilemma in a book I wrote this year that I was only able to resolve by incorporating this understanding into the text. Last year the editor and publisher Ginee Seo asked me to write a book on the Salem witch trials. The reading I had done on the period in graduate school gave me a sense of the approach I would take. Influenced by anthropology, new histories of witchcraft in Europe, and cross-cultural studies of magical practices, a generation of historians urged us to accept that the accused and the judges in Salem truly believed they were afflicted by witches. This effort to enter the worldview of the time was a counter to *The Crucible*, which rather directly applied psychological and social insights from the early fifties to the 1690s. I found this approach quite rich and fruitful, especially as it linked together history and folklore. The easiest way to enter the world of witches, I argue, is simply to read folktales and treat them as true.

But when I carefully read the records of the pretrial hearings that are our main source on the events, read some of the skeptical pieces written about them at the time, and, especially, read Bernard Rosenthal's thorough and relentlessly rational study *Salem Story*, I swung completely around. Rosenthal is a professor of English, not history, and he very carefully studied the original sources. With an almost lawyerly precision he pointed out the holes in the "belief-system" theory and insisted that the accusers were callous plotters who knew exactly what they were doing.

Most tellingly, he asked us to make sense of those moments when accusers claimed to have been tied up by spirits and later had to be cut down; when they claimed to receive bloody bites from specters, and demanded judges look at the teeth marks; when they were caught bringing a broken knife into court in order to claim it suddenly materialized there. In contrast to these strange manifestations, once a person confessed and in effect joined their side, the accusers were immediately able to stop all signs of affliction. Either they were actually attacked by demons, or they had to consciously stage these events. Without accepting Arthur Miller's Freudian views, Rosenthal gave us a Salem with characters quite as "evil" as those in the play.

The historian Mary Beth Norton is about to publish a new study of Salem entitled *In the Devil's Snare*, and I have had the good fortune to read it in a galley for a review I'll publish in the *LA Times*. She has some startling new insights to offer. The classic study of the trials, *Salem Possessed* by Paul Boyer and Stephen Nissenbaum, uncovered family tensions in the town and argued that the accusers were mouthpieces of those family dramas. Norton has focused on the accusers themselves and has discovered compelling evidence that they were traumatized by a particular set of Indian attacks in what is now Casco Bay, Maine. By researching the Maine and Indian threads—which had been essentially ignored before—she has reenvisioned the entire meaning of the trials. Her journey of discovery began when she treated the accusers as teenagers who spoke their own private agonies, not children ventriloquizing their fathers' public and political conflicts.

This is a valuable step, and notice that this historian's debate again turns on the question of the relationship of teenagers to their families. But I do not believe that we as adults, that the most diligent scholars, will ever be able to resolve the most fundamental question about Salem: were the accusers and judges in Salem driven by their beliefs and fears into some kind of hysterical state where they were imprisoned by their nightmares, or were they a group, a cabal, a coven if you will, of destructive individuals who cold-bloodedly chose to cause nineteen of their neighbors to be hanged? It is because I do not believe we can know the answer to this that I find all biological or medical theories, such as the psychedelic rotten wheat argument, implausible. How can you treat trial transcripts as medical records when you don't even know if you are reading about symptoms or theater? The confessions in Stalin's show trials were not due to bad vodka, but to his murderous designs and sadistic henchmen. The same may have been true in Salem.

Many, though not all, of the accusers were teenage girls. It seemed to me, then, that the best thing I could do in the book was to give my teenaged readers the evidence as I see it, and then to urge them to apply their own sense of psychology to the moment. They know how a group can be afflicted by fears and how real those fantasies can be. But they also know how a clique can turn into a vicious pack. They know with greater intensity than adults the idealistic impulse towards a cosmic sense of brotherhood as well as the compelling force of group identity that must discriminate between in and out, included and excluded, loved and hated. They know how loyalty to family and its mythologies is tested by loyalty to conscience and being truthful, and how being true to yourself can make you an outsider to your family, your peers, your community. In their daily lives, they are living the central dilemma of the Salem witch trials.

It is precisely for this reason that, in the end, I found Salem to be an inspiring story. I believe that it was individual devout Puritans speaking for themselves, for their own consciences, challenging their peers, their community, the most honored judges in the land, speaking at the cost of their own lives, who ended the trials. In a land ruled by Cain, the voice of Abel, of true faith, came in the voice of those confessed witches who recanted. They had made the successful transition out of the sick family to individual truth, and so were able to save their sisters' lives. Mary Easty admitted that her confession of being a witch was a lie, accepted that she would be killed for saying that, but, over and over, begged the judges that "no more innocent blood be shed." The greatest ministers in the land could not mistake the gravity, the sincerity, the truth of her words, and soon the trials stopped.

Am I my brother's keeper? Yes, if I am a self, if I have my own voice, if I am willing to trust my reason and my conscience against the lies and surreal dreams of the surrounding world. This is the last truth we adults have to give to younger readers, and our vehicle is the literature of adolescence. It is the reason for being of YA writing.

Making sense of the Salem trials requires knowledge of American history, but it is also a mystery that gets to the heart of that tangle of family and self, group pressure and self-definition, which is the essence of writing for teenagers. I think it requires a certain humility on our part as adult authors to let our teenage readers into the game. We need to honor them by treating them seriously, giving them access to the best adult historical detective work. But then we need to urge and inspire them to think for themselves.

In Liz Rosenberg's new novel, *17*, the main character, Steph, is teaching her fearful younger brother how to ride a bike. She runs after him as he shakily pedals, steadying and encouraging him. But at a point she lets him go on, and when he calls back "What are you holding on with?" she answers, "I'm holding on with my magic hand."

If brotherhood in the literature for young children can be expressed as a Silk Road of trade and commerce, in middle grade as an amalgam of the archetypical intensity of folktales and the new dynamics of blended families and mixed races, in high school it is an invisible hand. We shove our readers off to be individuals, to leave family behind, and yet we extend the grace of our knowledge, wit, imagination, and learning as lines that are there for them to grasp, if they want them. We have then completed the mission of literature for younger readers. By helping them to leave the immediate family, we welcome them into the family of adulthood, the true Family of Man.

Index

About the Author

Marc Aronson is book publisher and vice president of nonfiction content development at Carus Publishing. As an editor, he has worked with authors and artists such as Paul Fleischman, Nikki Giovanni, and Chris Raschka, and he developed and ran an imprint devoted to international and multicultural books for teenagers. Aronson is the author of *Art Attack: A Short Cultural History of the Avant-Garde* (Clarion, 1998) and the award-winning *Sir Walter Ralegh and the Quest for El Dorado* (Clarion, 2000) and *Exploding the Myths: The Truth about Teenagers and Reading* (Scarecrow Press, 2001). Aronson holds a doctorate in American history, where his specialty is the history of publishing. He frequently teaches courses on topics including children's publishing, publishing history, young adult publishing, electronic publishing, and publishing and diversity at the New York University Publishing Institute, Simmons College, and the Radcliffe Publishing Program. He lives in New Jersey with his wife.